IN SEARCH OF NORTH AMERICA

IN SEARCH
OF
NORTH
AMERICA

Reader's
Digest

PUBLISHED BY THE READER'S DIGEST ASSOCIATION LIMITED
LONDON NEW YORK MONTREAL SYDNEY CAPE TOWN

Originally published in partwork form,
Des Pays et des Hommes,
by Librairie Larousse, Paris

A Reader's Digest selection

IN SEARCH OF NORTH AMERICA

First English Edition Copyright © 1989
The Reader's Digest Association Limited, Berkeley Square House,
Berkeley Square, London W1X 6AB

Copyright © 1989
Reader's Digest Association Far East Limited
Philippines Copyright 1989
Reader's Digest Association Far East Limited

Originally published in French as a partwork,
Des Pays et des Hommes
Copyright © 1983
Librairie Larousse

Translated and edited by Toucan Books Limited, London
Translator: Kitty Black

Printed in Spain

Contents

COVER PICTURES

Top: *Monument Valley in Arizona. The stark desert landscape is punctuated by towering sandstone remnants rising from the valley floor.*

Bottom: *The Innuit, or Eskimos as they were previously known, are thought to have settled in the north of Canada and the United States some 4000 years ago.*

Lands of Opportunity

Oscar Wilde's quip on passing through customs, 'I have nothing to declare but my genius', might have applied not just to himself but also to the country he was entering: America. For, if genius is a capacity for unlimited invention, then America has it to the full.

It was, to begin with, a necessary quality. Without invention, and without the spirit of enterprise and the hard graft that goes with it, the great American adventure might never have taken off. Those first tiny colonies planted on the eastern seaboard of the New World found themselves in an environment that was rich and inviting, but a long way from home, exposed and challenging. The situation of the first colonists matches another from the other end of American history: the arrival of the first astronauts alone on the surface of the Moon.

The early Americans responded in a spirit which the entire country inherited. It was a spirit of adventurousness, of can-do, of get-up-and-go. And the direction they went was West, driving the frontier of American-ness ever farther into the continent that lay waiting for them. The frontier took a grip on the American imagination so that this, the leading-edge of the New World, became the symbol of the American dream. Daniel Boone, who blazed the trail through the Appalachians to the rich lands of Kentucky; Lewis and Clark exploring to the ocean shore of the Pacific North-West; the mountain men and pioneer farmers who followed them; the builders of the great trans-continental railroads and, perhaps above all, the cowboys – these people at the edge of the American civilisation became in some ways its central figures. The frontier has always been the main artery in America's idea of itself. When President Kennedy launched the great space drive of the 1960s, he tapped straight into that artery by treating space as the new frontier.

The genius of America has been to marry this dream to both the dollars and the dynamism that can make it happen. Unrivalled natural resources, the love of the new, the belief in a winner, hard-nosed good sense, a fair helping of ingenuity – these have turned America into a country of superlatives where, in the skyscraper, the great highway, the splendid car and the swimming-pooled suburbs, the dream has become manifest in material things.

But what is the essence of America? Many Americans, the most communicative people on earth, can only tell you what it is not.

It is not New York with its Aladdin's Cave shops, stone and glass canyons that alternatively boil and freeze, and its ghettos. Nor is it Los Angeles – 'several dozen suburbs in search of a city' – or the ravishing coast of California. San Francisco is too quirky; New Orleans, though it gave its music – jazz – to the world, is too colonial; while Nevada, where Las

Vegas and Reno blaze neon signs to the desert stars, is too brash. No one quite knows what to make of Florida, with its emerald and sapphire seas, its dripping swamps, space shuttles, Disney World, cheap resorts, rich mansions and hotels, and sky-high crime rate.

Neither is it Chicago, nicknamed 'The Windy City', with its Hollywood movie image of gangsters, underworld violence and political chicanery – an image of the past now, for today's city offers enough art, music and theatre to make it America's cultural runner-up to New York. Nor is it mighty Texas, land of oil barons – or so it might be imagined from the TV soap-opera image of the citizens of Dallas. Texas, annexed by congress in 1845 after nine years as an independent republic, has a distinctive character that serves as a reminder that the South once wanted to be its own country. A quarter bigger than France, and beset with a love of all things gigantic, Texas prompted John Steinbeck to call it a 'state of mind'.

The Old South is only now carving a new identity out of what was left by the Civil War of the last century. Not even New England, where the United States began, can be considered as typically American. The creeper-clad universities (hence Ivy League), the small ports, the 17th-century brick or white weather-boarded churches and villages seem instead a little wistful for the Old World – though at the same time declaring the traditional Yankee virtues of hard work and thrift.

Nevertheless, Americans will often confess to a single image. It is of a small town that so many city dwellers feel is waiting for them somewhere, complete with main street, courthouse, church, war memorial, barber shop, drug store, pretty houses surrounded by lawns, maybe a Civil War cannon, general store and, for convenience's sake, a supermarket and a fast-food restaurant facing a vast car park. It is likely to be somewhere in the Mid-West and is an America that is devoutly desired. In the words of a song from the musical *South Pacific*, it is 'as corny as Kansas in August, as normal as blueberry pie'.

Many aspects of Canada's history are similar to those of its neighbour. Like the United States, the frontier of Canada was driven westwards throughout the 19th century. And, as in the United States, this movement spawned a range of enduring images. Take the gold rush, for example, when 100,000 prospectors converged on Klondike in rusty steamboats or struggling over the daunting Chilkat Pass on foot, pared of all but their most essential tools and belongings which they carried on their backs.

In the two generations preceding the First World War, Canada discarded her status as a collection of rural colonies and emerged as a wealthy Western power. At the heart of this rapid transformation lay the development of the railroad. In 1885 the last spike of the Canadian Pacific Railway was driven into place. The first train left Montreal for British Columbia the following June. By extending the trade and industry of the St Lawrence valley westwards over the prairies, the Canadian Pacific Railway enmeshed the young country in a web of commerce.

Nevertheless, the two nations developed in different ways, with Canada, in some respects, overshadowed by its smaller neighbour (Canada is the second-largest country in the world after the USSR). Cars are still one of Canada's largest manufacturing industries; yet business strategy is supervised from Detroit. Overall, nearly half of Canada's manufacturing industry is owned by American firms.

Canada is changing fast, however. Although the country is still the greatest exporter of fish in the world and the largest exporter of pulp and newsprint, it is diversifying from its traditional industries. Modern Canada is as much a land of satellite dishes and giant hydro-electric schemes as of lumberjacks and Newfoundland fishermen. European visitors to Montreal are struck by the city's modernity as much as by its links to the past, with skyscrapers as well as vast subterranean walkways and galleries.

In Canada, individual freedom and minority cultures are treated with the same respect as the nation's economic health. There are, of course, the indigenous peoples. Most of the 286,000 registered Indians live in reserves in the west and north of the country, where many of them have kept their traditions and, in recent years, have taken much pride in asserting them. Living there brings certain inalienable rights, notably when it comes to hunting, fishing, taxes and education. There are also the Innuit, formerly called the Eskimos, who settled the mouth of the Mackenzie River, the Arctic islands and the north-eastern coastline as far south as Labrador.

The ancestors of many Westerners did not come from either Britain or France, the traditional sources of Canadian immigrants. The first immigrants to arrive in any numbers after the British were the Chinese, who worked as miners in the middle of the 19th century. As the trans-continental railway approached completion, many more were brought from their homeland to work as labourers on the line's construction. They stayed on to create Canada's largest Chinatown in Vancouver. In the vast influx during the twenty years before the First World War, families from the Ukraine, Germany and Iceland arrived in unprecedented numbers. As a result, the steepled churches of Scandinavia and central Europe became a new characteristic of the Canadian prairie horizon. In recent years, another influx from Asia has taken place, for Canada is one of the few Western countries to retain a liberal immigration policy.

United States of America

Life, liberty and the pursuit of happiness are among
the inalienable rights at the heart of the American Dream.
They form part of a vision that has beguiled millions since it
was given wings by the Declaration of Independence in 1776.
This vision has had its critics during the intervening couple of
hundred years, but its essence is indestructible,
and remains one of mankind's noblest concepts.

Previous page:
A galaxy of artificial stars illuminates the Los Angeles night, lighting the way home for movie superstars and Spanish-speaking farm workers alike.

Having starred in so many movies, it is no wonder that the Golden Gate Bridge is so famous and a recognisable symbol of San Francisco the world over. Every day it allows commuters easy access to the city from the north shore of the bay.

No other major American city is built on such a hilly site as San Francisco. Its contrasting ethnic districts are wrapped around the landscape so that you can walk through the Italian district and across to the Chinese, passing from one architectural style to another.

Way Out West

California is the sunshine state in which everything can be won by real effort and a good idea. Nevada is the place where two dice or a pack of cards can lose it all in five minutes. From the crystal breezes of the high Rockies to the oxygen masks of Los Angeles, from the stiff formality of Salt Lake City to the beach parties of Malibu, from the brutal reality of Death Valley to the ingenious fantasies of Disneyland, the American West has it all.

As in the rest of America, the distance between communities contributes much to this diversity. From Crescent City in the north to Tijuana over the Mexican border in the south, California stretches over 800 miles – the distance between John O'Groats and Land's End. From the Uinta Mountains in the north-east of Utah to the Gila Desert in the south-west of Arizona, there is a lot of space between townships. Faced with this immensity we are all pioneers in spirit, and whatever man does, nature will always have the last word.

The Pacific Coast Highway is the route with a view that carries the traffic from the foggy hills of San Francisco to the smoggy suburbs of Los Angeles and beyond. Running down the coast through Monterey and past the intimidating cliffs of Big Sur, its carriage-ways echo the winding curves of the shoreline and the famous Californian beaches. Many cars travelling south have surf-boards on their roof-racks and their occupants are still hoping to catch 'the big one', the wave that will carry the surfer from the open sea right up onto the beach. Others have trailers loaded with the hang-gliders that try to realise another fantasy of freedom. Up in the sky, these man-made seagulls soar effortlessly on the coastal breezes.

Cutting across the state, heading north-east from San Francisco to Reno in Nevada, the divorce capital of America – or from San Bernadino along Interstate 10, the freeway to Phoenix, Arizona – the gigantic trucks, a dazzling convoy of Kenworths and Macks, slug it out with the older, less glamorous railroads to carry the merchandise which is the backbone of American business. Their journeys are punctuated by billboards proclaiming the next 'Truck Stop' – the eating houses that can supply breakfast twenty-four hours a day.

Every stop is like the next, with a choice between fixed chromium stools set up against a curved bar or

Private enterprise is flexible enough to allow this 'Jesus freak' to operate his street stall selling slices of fresh pineapple on the same street that houses the office blocks containing America's giant corporations – all without any sense of conflict.

plastic seats at a plastic table. At any time of the day or night, a waitress will begin by bringing you a glass of iced water and then the menu, which will inevitably suggest eggs and bacon, ham or sausages, as well as pancakes or waffles, accompanied by a huge pot of coffee. Here, two truck drivers are arguing. One, a woman wearing a straw cowboy hat, the other, a man in a baseball cap, contest the merits of their respective headgear as protection against the sun. Their fellow travellers size them up, debating which is the owner of the black truck with its sides painted in orange, red and white flames. And what about its companion out front, the green truck whose radiator sports a realistic cobra's head with hypnotic eyes?

The waitress gives everybody more coffee. A customer asks if the earthquake on the news that morning had been a bad one. With a question like that, he must be from the East. The waitress looks at him, surprised, then turns to the truck drivers to see if they

The wooden houses of San Francisco are lovingly tended by their occupants. These examples of what might be called 'pioneer baroque' are not hidden away in a secluded suburb but nestle cheek-by-jowl with modern skyscrapers in the older parts of the city.

The climate of northern California is cooler than that of the south of the state, so the people of 'Frisco' only visit the beach in the spring and summer. The citizens of Los Angeles, however, can surf all year round in the sea off Santa Monica, Malibu or Long Beach.

Venice is a district where the mating ritual is conducted in all-American plumage. The concrete boardwalk, lined with cafés and fast food takeaways, becomes an arena for the fashions and passions of the local teenagers.

Even in Los Angeles there are still places where you can take your baby for a walk through up-market areas like Sunset Boulevard and sit down quietly to give him his bottle.

know anything about it. Oh yes. Near Santa Barbara? It was nothing. The truck driver with the baseball cap declares that Californians are not going to get worked up every time one of the 350 annual earthquakes is announced. The Easterner looks a little worried. He is obviously imagining that the notorious San Andreas faultline is about to open and swallow all California, burying him and his companions in the depths of the earth. After all, in 1906 the faultline ripped open and crossed San Francisco in a matter of seconds. He inevitably asks the obvious question: why do the Californians stay? The truck driver, pushing the peak of his cap back with his thumb, replies that California has everything: it may be half good and half bad, but half of California is better than all of Arizona. The traveller remarks that maybe tomorrow it will be a

different story. The drivers shrug and rise, pay their bills and separate. Where's the beef? What matters is here and now.

The couple sitting in the corner turn and follow the drivers with their eyes. Outside, the parked trucks roar into life. A seated woman looks at her husband and smiles. Yes, she was right. The woman in the straw sombrero has disappeared in a cloud of dust and painted flames.

Loaded with their cargoes of fruit and vegetables, the truckers do the return journey back to the big centres like San Francisco and Los Angeles. Freeway exits follow each other: Pasadena, Culver City, Beverly Hills, Venice, Hollywood. Two hours later you may still be on the highway looking for the Los Angeles exit. Where can it be in this bewildering

tangle of concrete packed with cars travelling nose to tail? In fact, it is all around; the urban sprawl, 170 miles north to south and much the same east to west, is without a specific centre to which the city's name can be attached.

With more than 7 million people to accommodate and no public transport worth discussing, the rush hour in this city becomes a survival course created to test the traveller's strength and endurance. Bumper to bumper, cars crawl along the concrete ribbon before finding their goal: a familiar exit. Most of the regulars in this daily ritual are fully prepared. Some open up folding tables and scribble a few notes for their next conference. Others watch the news on their TV sets. Some carry on long conversations over their in-car telephones. Of course, every car is equipped with a

Built on the outskirts of Los Angeles, Disneyland provides an amusement park where mythological European symbols, like the double-headed eagle of Austria, mix with the brilliant inventions of Walt Disney's animation artists. The park emphasises the optimism of childhood.

stereo. And so they all relax on the motorway for at least an hour and a half, each driver sitting alone among thousands of others.

Outside the cars, the sun is turning their exhaust fumes into a tasty cocktail. Los Angeles is sandwiched between the cool currents of the Pacific and a range of mountains, behind which is a desert. Warm air rolls off the hills and traps the cooler air underneath, forming a very stable series of layers. As a result the city has a much lower average wind speed than any other metropolitan area in North America, so all those fumes just stagnate. However, car emission regulations are now becoming very stringent in the United States and the problem will soon begin to recede, although it will never entirely vanish.

California is a state that threatens to be submerged by its own success. In 1845, just before it came under American control, it had about 5000 citizens, of whom probably fewer than 400 were of European extraction. Five years later the world's first great gold-rush had changed all that, and by 1860 there were 380,000 inhabitants. But it was the arrival of the trans-continental railway that made the difference in the long term.

The connection to the markets of the East encouraged farmers to settle in the central valley area, which stretches over 400 miles from Red Bluff in the north, past Sacramento to Bakersfield in the south, not far from Los Angeles. Much of this valley is very dry, particularly in the south. So the first farmers grew barley, which needs little water, or raised cattle, which can endure arid conditions. Then, in 1881, technology took a hand when Andrew Chase invented the refrigerated railway wagon to carry meat from Chicago to Boston. This invention was soon applied to

A Disneyland star, one of Snow White's seven dwarfs, welcomes children to a world in which being small is no disadvantage. The Disney Corporation is in the happy position of having characters who need never tire or get sick. The person under the mask can easily be substituted without children or parents being any the wiser.

vegetables and fruit, which yield enough profit to make large-scale irrigation worth while.

Nowadays, California has one of the most extensive and sophisticated water storage and delivery systems in the world, with canals and aqueducts stretching hundreds of miles. Over 8 million acres yield a wide variety of crops that could not flourish without a supply of water that is just a telephone call away. Some, like oranges, lemons and the grapes that make the wine, are always associated with California. More surprising is the state's most valuable crop – cotton. In the early 1980s, California produced more cotton

The days when the sight of an ankle was something shocking seem as remote as the Stone Age but such attitudes were still current when the grandmothers of these young women were growing up – especially if they lived in the West.

than any other state in the country.

Most of these crops are processed and packed very close to fields that produce them, to ensure maximum freshness. Many of the workers who tend the crops and man the plants are Spanish-speaking Americans, known as Latinos or Chicanos, or even illegal immigrants from Mexico. Of course, California once belonged to Mexico, and over 90 per cent of its small population was Spanish-speaking at that time. But the balance changed very noticeably during the second half of the 19th century as the state began to develop.

Driving through Sequoia National Park at the foot of Mount Whitney, the visitor is surrounded by these enormous conifers, which can grow as high as 250 feet. They live for thousands of years because their trunks are full of resins that resist decay.

From the first, Californian agriculture depended on immigrant labour: Chinese, Japanese and Filipino, as well as Mexican, simply because the wages have always been appallingly low. Since 1945 immigration across the Mexican border has turned into a flood, whatever American officials have done to stop it, and by 1988 children of European stock were in a minority in Californian schools.

This cultural shift is reflected in the shops and restaurants of the region. Mexican food, like tacos and enchiladas – a mixture of meat, cheese and chili served in a pancake made of maize flour – is very popular. Small shops are stuffed with crucifixes, rosaries, statues of the Virgin and assorted saints spilling over onto the pavements. Most of the billboards, posters and public announcements are written in English and Spanish.

Of course, California is not just the number one agricultural state in the union: it is also number one in

manufacturing – an extraordinary combination that is quite unlike the economy of any other part of the country. It was the discovery of oil in southern California at the end of the 19th century that set the ball rolling. Nowadays, four of the ten most productive oilfields in the United States are found in the region, while offshore drilling promises even greater riches. The First World War stimulated growth in the state's industrial production, as it did for the rest of the country. At the same time the arrival of the movie industry, previously based in the New York area, changed the state's image in the eyes of America and the rest of the world. The 1930s saw the development of California into one of the world's leading aircraft manufacturing centres. After 1945, this industry was slowly transformed into aerospace, which in turn spawned other affiliated industries, like computers and electronics, that grew to independence in the decades that followed.

All this activity has placed more and more pressure on the resources of southern California. More people need more homes, while more factories and more roads use more land. This pushes even highly profit-able farms and orchards onto marginal land that needs more water to be productive. Orange Country, for instance, used to produce what its name suggests; but more profit could be made by selling the land to developers and today Orange County is just another piece of the urban sprawl. Unfortunately, the extra irrigation that the move to more marginal land demands is not easily available. Already some of the state's former allocation of the waters of the Colorado River has been redirected to the Central Arizona Project. The only large source of fresh water on America's West Coast that is still under-exploited is the Columbia River, but that is in the state of Washington, 600–700 miles north of the areas that need irrigating.

This luxury house in Palm Springs is a fine example of the international style of architecture developed in Europe in the 1920s, which spread to the United States in the following decade when architects fled from Hitler. The clean lines and elegant proportions were inspired by Japanese domestic architecture. It became fashionable in the West because the warm climate favours the relaxed integration of gardens and interiors.

Gold was found in 1848 in the American River in California, and a rush to make a quick fortune began. But the promises of the first mines quickly faded, leaving only a few rusty and abandoned tools as reminders of the efforts made in the mountains of the Far West.

Small towns like Bodie, California are reminders of what life was like at the time of the first great gold-rush.

A place to lose your heart

Northern California is the antithesis of the southern half of the state. Where Los Angeles has car parks, the north has national parks. Where the south is hot and full of people, the north is misty and full of trees. Linking the two is the Golden Gate Bridge, which was suspended among the clouds by engineers who had skill and imagination. Nowadays it has few rivals as an elegant commuter route, while as a setting for movie thrillers or police melodramas it is a prime contender for the number one slot – the most beautiful bridge in the world.

At its southern end is one of the few cities in North America that looks as though it is older than yesterday. San Francisco received its first European visitors in 1769, when a Spanish expedition trekking north from Mexico got lost. Like so much of the Californian coastline, it became the site of a Catholic mission.

But until the gold-rush of 1849, the settlement on the rim of one of the world's greatest natural harbours was no more than a village with just a few hundred inhabitants. Then, in little more than a year, its population grew to 56,000.

When the first trains from the East arrived in 1869, the city seemed to have an unlimited tomorrow. Even the disaster of 1906, in which a fire ravaged the buildings shattered by the earthquake, failed to blight the city's prospects; the quality of the harbour and the fertile soil of the Sacramento Valley north-east of the city saw to that. But if Frisco was growing, LA was growing faster and the economic balance of the state tilted towards the south.

Today, the city on the bay has its bankers, tourists and civil servants to keep it warm. At eight o'clock in the morning the traffic begins its daily surge from the 'burbs' to the downtown area. Business in Montgomery Street, the most important financial centre in the West, is brisk until midday; then, after a short lunch break, it continues until six. Meanwhile, amid the reflecting glass of the office blocks, you can watch the ancient tramways trundling up and down the steep

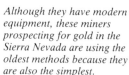
Although they have modern equipment, these miners prospecting for gold in the Sierra Nevada are using the oldest methods because they are also the simplest.

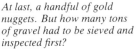
At last, a handful of gold nuggets. But how many tons of gravel had to be sieved and inspected first?

The grey squirrel can be found throughout North America. Because it is very flexible about food, it has spread from the forests into towns, where it is treated with a tolerance that human beings have never shown to its cousin the rat.

*In 1850 Las Vegas was only a
small village, an oasis in the
desert on the way to
California. The arrival of the
railway in 1905 made a
considerable difference.
During the 1930s, Nevada
changed its gambling laws
and the oasis disappeared
under asphalt when the first
casino came to town.
Everything here, from the
lights to the free
entertainment, is devoted to
making more money.*

streets. Scattered across the slopes, the small, painted
wooden houses seem to offer a cosy welcome and
invite you to make yourself at home.

To stay cool and do your own thing is the real motto
of the San Franciscan. If you take a walk along
Fisherman's Wharf, originally a tiny fishing port,
nibbling a few shrimps, a bag of chips or some
'veggies' – raw mushrooms, avocado pear, chick peas
and bean sprouts – you may suddenly come upon a
street entertainment: a girl blowing a trumpet while a
man in a black and white clown's make-up caricatures
the latest events on the American political scene. At
the end of the jetty a young executive, briefcase in
hand, is standing quite still, his eyes fixed on the deep
waters of the bay, with a sort of pyramid-shaped
dunce's cap on his head. He has been assured this will

put him in touch with the spiritual forces of ancient
Egypt. Nobody pays the least attention.

Eccentricity is tolerated in California partly
because nobody can tell when it is going to turn into
a moneymaking proposition. In the autumn of 1976, a
21-year-old with shoulder-length hair, cut-off jeans
and sandals was working away with a friend in a
garage in Los Altos, which is about halfway between
San Francisco and San Jose. He had got it into his
head that people would be prepared to buy a computer that was small enough to sit on a desk top, which
sounded like a strange idea to most people in 1976.
Seven years later, Steve Jobs' holding of stock in
Apple Corporation, the company that he and his
friend founded, was worth 284 million dollars and the
company was among the 500 largest in the world.

There are many stories of individual success among the people who live and work in Silicon Valley, which is not a valley at all but a plain sandwiched between the Los Altos Hills and the southern end of San Francisco Bay. It was given its nickname in 1971 by a journalist who wanted a label for an area which was rapidly becoming the centre of the world's electronics industry. This strip of land 30 miles long and 10 miles wide has given the world pocket calculators, video games, home computers, cordless telephones and digital watches, all of which are based on the silicon microprocessing chips from which the area gets its name. Such success has given those that work in the area the highest average incomes in the USA for any such region and over 15,000 millionaires live in the northern third of the Valley.

At the weekend, thousands desert California's asphalt and neon to relax in the mountains of the Sierra Nevada, among the family crowds in Disneyland or on one of the many beaches that speckle the coastline. However, any expectation that Californian energy is about to subside is misplaced. The promenades and the sand are just another venue for the sunshine masquerade: gyrating on skateboards, dancing on roller-skates and abandoned to the rhythms of Walkmans. Here, the sunset is always red.

Once the sun has slipped away, the neon signs on Sunset Boulevard down the coast in LA reappear to infect the sky with their own brand of glamour. 'The Strip' has its own rhythm, changing according to each particular district, but it always has a beat. This is the kingdom of music, cinema and television in which Hollywood is just the most famous suburb.

In the background, standing in the back of a stationary truck, a man holds up a huge placard saying 'Act naturally'. Immediately, twenty man-sized tubes of toothpaste appear and begin to walk among the crowd, stopping now and then to shake a friendly hand. Three minutes later, a director yells 'Cut – thanks everyone!' and the television crew dole out free passes to Disneyland to all the people who have taken part in the commercial. In Europe it would attract a crowd. Here it's just part of the cabaret.

No wonder they call it 'glitter gulch': 43 miles of neon lighting and 2 million light bulbs are popping away to entice visitors into these temples of chance. Nowadays the city has to try harder, for the success of Atlantic City, which gets 50 per cent more visitors every year than its Western rival, has started to give several other resorts ideas about ways to restore their flagging revenues.

Although it has little more than 200,000 permanent inhabitants, Las Vegas is visited by more than 16 million tourists a year. Many come to be either married or divorced in a state which makes both easy. Couples can choose from over 140 churches or small chapels that are frequently open 24 hours a day.

Sequins in the desert

The cheapest way to get to Las Vegas is by bus. Every afternoon one leaves Los Angeles and gets to the neon oasis in the early evening. These chrome-trimmed metallic monsters are solidly built with square corners and tinted windows. Each stop is either built like a railway station, designed to meet the traveller's every need, or a mere pull-in, marked by a pole on an isolated roadside where a few locals wait to climb on board and travel the short distance to their destination. They join the curious mixture of inquisitive first-timers and blasé regulars, all intent on a good time across the state line. The sun sets just as Interstate Highway 15 reaches the desert, a desolate area reminiscent of the dark side of the moon. The vast empty landscape slides silently past. It is hard to realise that you are still passing through the most populous state in the country.

The driver announces over the intercom that you have reached Nevada and the bus rushes on through total darkness. Nothing cuts the night until the lights of Las Vegas are suddenly upon you. Two women sitting behind the driver are chatting. One, a blue-rinsed grandmother, has large, sun-burned, wrinkled hands. She emphasises her words by pushing her glasses up and down on her nose. Her younger neighbour is wearing jeans and a brightly coloured shirt patterned with fruit. The older woman explains how she arrived here originally from New York as a young bride, to raise cattle and live on a small ranch. Her companion asks if you can still see the mustangs, the famous wild horses? With a sudden flash of pleasure shining in her eyes, the elderly settler describes how, not long ago, she had been riding in the desert hills when she came across just such a herd under some trees. At first they just trotted away but then they quickened their pace until, without warning, they all broke into a gallop and disappeared over the horizon in a cloud of dust. 'No one can know what the word freedom means until they have seen these horses galloping along, without saddle, bridle or bit.' The driver adds that in the old days the mustangs were killed for dog food, but that they are now protected by law.

The bus pulls up at a quiet unpretentious station. Alongside the baggage claim is a line of slot machines – the one-armed bandits of Las Vegas. The fabulous gambling strip is just round the corner and as you cross the road you are overwhelmed by the neon flashing in every conceivable colour. Some light up as others go out, others flash on and off continuously or seem to be pulling a long thread around an invisible design. Every casino seems named to offer opulence without parallel: the Golden Nugget, Caesar's Palace. Every door seems permanently open. From these cathedrals of chance comes an electronic sirens' song – the cry of pain from the one-armed bandit that is forced to yield a few coins in order to encourage the other gamblers or attract passers-by.

Each casino looks different but feels the same. As the handles turn and the machines clatter into action, you can hear the owner making his profit. Drinks are usually free to gamblers because it encourages the public to spend more. The bars are usually at the far end of the room, and to quench your thirst you have to run the gauntlet of unprecedented opportunity. Once past the roulette tables, the blackjack dealers and the faro wheels, you can drink the biggest and cheapest cocktails in America if you do not want to play the tables. Every year 16 million visitors come to this town in the middle of nowhere; its best-known neighbour is the atomic weapons testing area to the north-west whose work sometimes gives the casinos a gentle nudge and makes the chandeliers rattle.

Between two hotly contested games of pool, the saloon is still the favourite watering hole where the cattle ranchers of Tombstone, Arizona can 'chew the fat'.

One of the bus passengers decides to risk a small sum, just to see what it's like. He reaches into his pocket for change and a hostess is immediately at his side. Soon his coin is in the slot and he is pulling the handle. The cylinders with pictures of fruit whirl into action then bump to a halt. No luck this time. There's no harm in another go. Fifteen minutes later he has lost 50 dollars and his wife is grateful that it's time to get back on the bus. As he leaves he passes a huge machine that accepts 20 dollar bills. His wife breathes a sigh of relief as the bus speeds on into the night.

The Promised Land

Salt Lake City is beautifully laid out at the foot of the Wasatch Mountains. In fact, everything is as it should be. The streets cross at right-angles and the buildings are simple squares or rectangles. The avenues are lined with trees, flowerbeds are square and uniformly planted, everything is just so.

At the city's centre rise the six grey spires of the Mormon Temple. Nearly half of the population of the city (and 70 per cent of the State of Utah) are members of the Church of Jesus Christ of Latter-day Saints and follow a strict moral code which discourages tobacco, alcohol or any stimulant such as tea or coffee. The majority give 10 per cent of their wages to the work of the church. Mormon guides keep an eye out for tourists and will invite you to a.tour of Temple Square. They take anyone who accepts to the visitors' centre, opening the door with a magnetic key rather like a banker's card.

The site of the city was chosen in 1847 by the Church's leader, Brigham Young, after the Mormons had travelled across the Mid-West, searching for a place they could call home. After the harassment of their early years, they wanted a spot where they could practice their faith without interference.

Unlike the neighbouring states where the inhabitants try to profit from the present, Utah is concerned with the future, which is why the majority who subscribe to the 'Book of Mormon' have underground stores that could support the whole population for a year. The Mormons plan to survive any catastrophe. Perfectly organised, they represent a major force in the American economy.

But even this orderly society has produced some notorious outlaws, like Butch Cassidy, the son of a Mormon preacher, and his partner, the Sundance Kid. After one of their spectacular hold-ups they took refuge in the fabulous Bryce Canyon, whose steep precipices in a more isolated part of the state provided a perfect hideout.

Religious toleration is at the heart of American society and different groups are found in every state. But none is more extraordinary than the Church of Jesus Christ of Latter-day Saints: the Mormons. In search of their promised land they trekked 1000 miles before they founded Salt Lake City in the desert at the foot of the Wasatch Mountains. The headquarters of the church is still to be found here.

Making a reservation

The vast region which includes southern Utah, the south-west of Colorado, New Mexico and Arizona forms a geographic unity where only the Indians are really at home. It is a landscape that, only with difficulty, can be shaped to the requirements of modern man. Yet for the people of the Indian nations, the Pueblo, Hopi, Apache and Navajo, it has been home for centuries. Indeed, when the Spanish first entered the region, it held the most concentrated population of Indians north of Mexico, despite the dry conditions and the lack of game to hunt. This was possible because irrigated agriculture had been practised by some Indians for many centuries.

Because they possessed land that was so inhospitable to European settlers, many groups, such as the Hopi in northern Arizona, live on reservations that are situated where their people have always lived. Today the Indians of New Mexico and Arizona control 27 million acres on which 270,000 of their people live.

The Pueblo village of Taos in New Mexico, for example, with its adobe houses, is still inhabited by the descendants of its original settlers and life goes on calmly in the homes that have not changed for generations. The mud houses make flowing patterns that mingle with the neighbouring hills; few have either electricity or running water as their occupants prefer to maintain their traditional way of life.

In the surrounding arid land, the soil is often intensely coloured. It was here that the first face in the world was painted, say the Indians, meaning the face of the earth, the painted desert. The colours of the shale run from ochre through white to blue, pale green, mauve and turquoise, and are particularly vivid in the clear desert air. To European settlers, these vast open spaces represented a daunting challenge.

In the feverish days of the Californian gold-rush, the pioneers had to overcome many obstacles such as deserts, dry valleys and the first great barrier that blocked their path, the great chain of the Rocky Mountains, the second longest range in the world, which runs from Alaska to New Mexico. Today, the Rockies are again a testing ground, this time in the clash between conservationists and new prospectors. On this occasion the quest for mineral wealth is not conducted by hapless individuals but by giant corporations who employ geologists, satellite surveys and the best technology they can afford. For, although the dry soil is discouraging to the farmer, large deposits of coal, oil, natural gas, uranium and copper have been discovered beneath the surface. This has been good news for the Navajo in particular and their share of the profits from the exploitation of their reservation comes to over 100 million dollars a year. This capital has been invested in factories built on the reservation and Navajo women can now be found assembling electronic components in the repeatedly filtered, dust-free air of 'clean rooms', which are so essential in the manufacture of microchips.

On the neighbouring plains, the Indians' eternal adversary of the silver screen, the cowboy, has not done quite so well and, even if he has kept his wide-brimmed hat and high-heeled boots, he has become just another employee on the corporate ranch, raising cattle and working under orders. Only in the north-west of the country can ranch hands still be found who retain yesterday's freedom.

One of the annual events of the south-west is the great inter-tribal festival at Window Rock, a small village in Arizona near the border with New Mexico. A large number of Indians take part, but there are also plenty of tourists who come to watch. Thousands of cars and trucks arrive from every direction. Many Indians bring their tepees, which they

Rodeos have become a ritual that bears only a slight resemblance to skills necessary on the modern ranch. No one would try to ride a full-grown steer outside the ring, but that is what carries the most prestige at every event.

Under the wide-brimmed hats, men, boys and even very small children watch the rodeos. During the summer they are the most popular events in the towns of the American West.

After the frustrations of working in an office, an opportunity to let off steam is something most people grasp with open arms. Dressing up as cowboys and reliving the 'good old days' in a reconstructed 19th-century town is one of the more unusual ways that Americans can relax.

will erect a little away from the busiest centres. These tepees might look fragile because they are little more than a cloth stretched over wooden poles, but they are really very strong. The framework consists of 12 or 15 poles carefully cut and arranged to lean against each other to make a conical structure. This was originally covered with bison skins but these days heavy cloth is used. A cord tied to one of the poles is used to raise the covering and allow the smoke to escape from the small fire that is lit inside the tent. These tepees are the traditional tents of the nomadic tribes who hunted for their food and never developed a settled agriculture like the Pueblo. However, at these annual festivals they have now become convenient accommodation for visiting Indians who prefer adobe houses on their home territory.

During the fair everyone displays their hand-made rugs, baskets and pottery or the animals they have reared. Buying, selling and bartering flourish. It is also the time for the Indians to wear their finest clothes. Men and women put on silver necklaces studded with turquoises, heavy belts embossed with beautifully carved ornaments and headbands of narrow leather thongs covered with white, blue,

orange, yellow and black beads worked into traditional geometric patterns.

When darkness falls, drums are arranged in circles. The dancers fasten bracelets of bells to their wrists and ankles and wear bunches of feathers on their shoulders or on their heads. A dance for the children begins. Around the same big drum, six drummers, each using their own drumsticks, beat out the rhythm set up by their colleagues. Very young dancers, some only five years old, hop clumsily from foot to foot, while teenagers spin round imitating the flight and bobbing motion of birds, sometimes barely touching

Between the states of Utah, Arizona and New Mexico lie the reservations of the Hopi, Zuni, Navajo and Apache Indians. Many of them have turned to breeding sheep in the magnificent setting of Monument Valley.

For rodeos and 'pow-wows', Indians dress in traditional costumes, displaying the unique characteristics of each tribe in their clothing, jewellery and weaving. These Zuni women carry the pottery, with its distinctive motifs, for which they are renowned.

the ground, sometimes stamping heavily. The drums strike up a faster beat and the musicians begin to sing and encourage the dancers to establish the rhythm of the dance. Soon everyone is invited to join in and form a circle of dancers, one behind the other, all around the drums. Men and women follow each other, using the same rhythm but making free and individual movements. Some wear leather and multi-coloured feather ornaments, others are in T-shirts and jeans; the atmosphere is relaxed and informal.

At the end of a week the Indians return to the reservations where the Navajo, Pueblo and Hopi live and where many pursue the traditional crafts which have become famous, attracting thousands of visitors every year. The Indians consider that the craftsman puts some of his creative power into every object he makes. So he must always make a deliberate mistake somewhere, either in the design or by adding a different coloured thread to the woven blanket, so that his spirit can escape and not be imprisoned by his own work.

However, the American West is not just about tradition. In the transformation that has overtaken American society during the last generation, as old industries die and new ones are born, there has been a steady movement away from the old industrial heartland towards the south and the south-west. Nevada and Arizona are among the fastest-growing states in the country, while cities like Phoenix and Tucson now have a population that is over seven times the size it was in 1945.

Now that the summer heat has been conquered by

After being pushed further and further west, on to poorer and poorer land, the Indian population was reduced to about 200,000. But they have now bounced back to nearly 800,000. The majority live in reserves, spread over 24 states, mostly in the South and North-West.

The Navajo are such fine weavers that some of their baskets can hold water. Yet each piece of work contains a deliberate mistake so that the creative spirit of the weaver is not imprisoned in perfection.

air-conditioning, developing companies have been keen to exploit the open space of the south-west. Foremost amongst these have been those involved in the electronics and aerospace industries. Over 70 per cent of these companies based in Arizona are clustered around Phoenix which, with its surrounding suburbs, is home to over half the state's citizens.

A settlement first appeared in the area in 1868 and by 1870 it was being called after the legendary bird. The relatively rich agricultural land surrounding Phoenix attracted a steady stream of settlers in the decades that followed and they developed an irrigation system that helped them to prosper. The local Indian population had grown an unusual type of cotton bush that produced long strands of the fibre for centuries before settlers arrived. When the car industry began to develop during the early years of this century, tyre manufacturers realised that this 'long staple' cotton was an ideal material to incorporate into their product. During the boom years of the First World War Goodyear began buying large tracts of land in the area and by 1920 owned 230,000 acres of cotton. However, the price of cotton collapsed in 1921 and the company began to dispose of its property. When the price later recovered, local farmers tried the crop, importing pickers from the deep south.

The big change came to Arizona during the Second World War when an old army base in the south-east of the state, Fort Huachuca, was turned into the army's Electronic Proving Ground. When the electronics industry started to take off in the 1950s, it was not surprising that they chose to establish themselves near to one of their largest customers.

Arizona's other big dollar earner is tourism, for one of America's great natural attractions is situated in the north-west of the state. The Grand Canyon is about 200 miles long, 5000 feet deep and varies from 5 to 10 miles wide. As the surrounding plateau was gradually raised by geological action during the last 10 million years, the Colorado River cut into it, exposing the layers of rock that can now be seen from the canyon lip by visitors to this isolated area.

To escape and to stay free: that is the strongest tradition of the American West. In the 19th century, the settlers came in covered waggons and spent months travelling and risking their lives to make a new start with new horizons. Nowadays they come in jumbo jets or pick-up trucks. The dangers may have disappeared but the intention is still the same. The West today is what it was yesterday: America's frontier of opportunity.

The rapids on the great Colorado River rush down the gorges of the Grand Canyon, and there are more than 120 miles of falls, white water and treacherous rocks to negotiate. But such a challenge only acts to goad the intrepid canoeists to test their skill on the ancient river.

The Last Pioneers

On a small ranch in Montana, it is 11 am and time to think about brunch. Even though it is Sunday, Roy and his wife Jean have already spent three and a half hours in the stockyard separating the cows in calf from the rest of the herd. Like many other local farmers, they raise cattle as well as sheep: 'It's all good sense, you never know.' They take off their rubber boots, heavy with stockyard mud, and change into their riding boots on the porch.

Out front, the first pick-up truck arrives with Roy's sister Charlene at the wheel. She raises cattle on her own spread over the state line in Wyoming. He has invited her for a Sunday meal which seems to hover somewhere between breakfast and lunch. Here in the North-West brunch has its own particular flavour, just like the people.

The states of Wyoming, Montana, Idaho, Oregon and Washington were among the last in the USA to be settled. In 1959 they were joined by Alaska which had to wait over 90 years before it was granted full statehood after its purchase from the Russians in 1867. The population of the six states that form the North-West is a little bigger than that of Greater London, although the area is almost eight times the size of Britain. Since the population is so spread out it is hardly surprising that they tend to go their own way, isolated as they are from both central government and the other communities of the United States.

North-Westerners live either in small towns or on small ranches, and the only cities of any size are Seattle, Washington's major harbour, and Portland in Oregon. Not only was the territory among the last to be settled, but those who chose the area brought different attitudes and different expectations with them. In the south-west the pioneers dreamed of becoming rich overnight, so towns sprang up and died around the various mines. Nature was despoiled and exploited before people moved on, not caring about the mess they left behind them. The North-West offered different resources and the settling of its lands followed a different scale of values. This is the fundamental reason why North-Westerners were among the first in the United States to become environmentally conscious. They wish to nurture their wilderness of vast impenetrable forests, boiling lakes and geysers. So, it is no surprise that the North-West was the site of the world's first national park.

Huge forests stretch as far as the eye can see across Montana, Wyoming and Idaho, providing shelter for the herds of elk. Yellowstone National Park sits astride the three states, covering an area of 3472 square miles.

Saving Old Faithful

The soft spring breeze whispers through the leaves of the aspens, with their dappled trunks and delicate foliage running the gamut of greens and golds, on the lower slopes of the Rocky Mountains. Their shadow in summer and their layer of fallen leaves in winter protect the young pine saplings which in 50 years' time will have grown into a new forest among the foothills, clothing the valleys, river banks and mountain clefts and climbing the mountains themselves.

In the sub-alpine climate of Yellowstone National Park, the sparkling transparent streams are full of rainbow trout. Black bears amble along their banks and stop above a rocky pool, one paw raised, to catch a fish, using their claws like large hooks. Fallow deer spring away and hide in the undergrowth, and the tourists can feast on blueberries and whortleberries. Many other animals, unknown in Europe, can easily appear around the next bend in the path: a skunk, for instance, whose black fur is banded with a broad white stripe that runs from its nose to the end of its bushy tail. If it is startled, it sprays a highly pungent secretion to deter the molester. Sheltering under immense waterfalls, a small herd of wild sheep stops for a moment before taking flight, leaping from rock to rock with breathtaking agility.

To enjoy these sights you must leave the only regular highway which winds through the park and set

off on foot, well equipped and observing all the signs counselling caution. Furthermore, it is essential that pedestrians take care to avoid all the forbidden areas or at least proceed only in the company of a qualified guide. This is no safari park.

One way to enjoy the park involves a five-day trip on horseback, starting on the east bank of Yellowstone Lake and ending on the Continental Divide, or maybe the high peaks of the Grand Teton Range. This trek takes a group through prairies echoing with the hooves of deer, over the wooded slopes, through dark forests of spruce and pine and on to a high plateau still covered by snow in the middle of August. Even though it is still an adventure, this trip will not involve any unnecessary risks and the riders will be more than satisfied with finding a tuft of blue columbines in a rocky cleft.

Some sections of the park have never been disturbed by humans; this means that some species can be protected which, at the beginning of the century, were hunted to provide trophies for people unconcerned with the true value of wildlife. A number of grizzly bears and pumas survive in the remoter areas, while brown and black bears wander freely over hundreds of miles, even though this poses certain problems in the more popular areas.

Perhaps Yellowstone's greatest attraction and the reason Congress voted to preserve it back in 1872 are its 200 geysers, the world's largest concentration of

Conditions for raising cattle in the North-West are excellent, in spite of the harsh winters. The ranches are of medium size and are normally operated as a family business. Mutual help among farmers is an important feature in the region.

Women worked as hard as the men on the frontier. The same is probably true of their descendants, though modern technology has lightened their load considerably and large families are now exceptional. The women of Wyoming were the first in the world to win the right to vote – in 1869.

The cattle of Montana are rounded up in the spring for branding. Each animal is lassoed and tied to the saddle, then held while it is branded with a hot iron. This makes it easier for its owner to identify it should it go astray.

Ranching traditions are very strong in Wyoming, despite the passage of time and the arrival of new generations. These links with the past are visible in the clothes, the music and the decoration of the ranches.

Ringling, in Montana, is a typical small town of the American North-West: it has one street boasting the bank, the drugstore-grocery and the saloon, which doubles as a hotel-restaurant for long-distance truck drivers.

these small spouts of boiling water. In addition, the area is overflowing with small hot springs which heat up the waters of the lakes and mud craters. The most spectacular geyser is Old Faithful, which blows about 7500 gallons of boiling water high into the air every hour. Spectators wisely stand a safe distance away or take shelter if they are down wind when the eruption occurs. From the day it was discovered over 100 years ago, Old Faithful has never failed to blow a misty vapour into the blue sky above Wyoming on schedule.

Meanwhile, back across the state line, brunch is getting under way at Roy and Jean's. The trucks are pulled up in front of the porch and parked like horses, without any attempt at organisation. Montana number plates include the name of the state followed by the slogan: 'Big sky'. The Wyoming plates carry 'The Cowboy State' under a picture of a bucking bronco. Most of the pick-ups have racks in the back holding shot-guns for a coyote hunt, which has been scheduled to follow the meal, because these predators have been attacking the sheep.

The wooden ranch house is typical of similar buildings in Montana, Idaho, Wyoming and eastern Washington. Most have the same short flight of steps leading up to a porch surrounded by a balustrade. On summer evenings everyone enjoys the cool air, sitting on the planks bleached grey by the elements. There is a splendid view of the high prairies, golden with ripening corn or green with grass, whose rolling distances seem to push the horizon farther and farther away and stretch the immensity of the blue sky even more. On such mellow evenings, not a house or a vehicle can be seen. The only features that disrupt the undulating landscape are the ochre-coloured sides of some far-off cliffs, pierced by the caves which provide shelter for the coyotes and other animals.

The ranchhouse is painted yellow with white trimmings and has oil-fired central heating to cope with the long, tough winters, although many of the neighbouring farms still use stoves that burn wood or sawdust bricks if they are near enough to forests and sawmills. The windows on the north side are double-glazed against the cold winds.

Charlene has brought steaks as her contribution to brunch, which will be finished off with tall glasses of home-produced milk and blueberry muffins.

(American muffins are small, individual sponge cakes and are not meant to be toasted.) Sitting round the huge table in the main living room everyone is wearing denim, which got its name because the cloth was originally woven in Nîmes in France. The men sport huge belt buckles, many of which were won at rodeos.

The walls of the farm, like those of most hotels and bars roundabout, are hung with reproductions of the works of Charles M. Russell, a Montana painter who was born in 1880 and produced more than 3000 paintings of scenes of the daily life of the West. In his pictures Russell expressed his love for the rough and independent life of the cowboys, showing them invading the local bars, bringing the stockyard mud in on their boots, Stetsons crammed down over uncombed hair, wearing filthy shirts. They were and still are the same, surviving well into the 20th century, proud of their way of life, telling real or imaginary stories of hard times in the mountains and prairies where everything is a constant struggle: against the cold in winter and the heat in summer, against coyotes if they are looking after sheep, and always against the loneliness.

The farms are usually many miles apart and each has to be as self-supporting as possible. A constant watch has to be kept, counting and recounting the herds. In the winter, supplementary feeding has to be

Hunting, which is strictly controlled, is authorised only in certain regions during specified periods and for plentiful species, such as caribou. In autumn the hunters gather in Idaho where the best stocks of deer and antelope are to be found. Armed with powerful rifles with telescopic sights, they rarely miss the target.

The western saddle is very heavy when compared to its English counterpart. The rider is firmly supported and can work long hours in reasonable comfort.

organised: tractors are driven to the snow-covered grazing grounds and hay spread for the red mass of cattle clustered around the trailer, lifting up their white heads. Herefords are the most popular breed in Wyoming and Montana because of their hardiness and the quality of their meat.

The discovery that Montana was cattle-raising country is said to have occurred around 1860. According to legend, a rancher decided to take his cattle and leave Texas because it was getting too crowded and too civilised for his taste. He drove his herd north where he had heard that there were endless plains, with grass as high as a man and peopled by Indians who called it 'the end of the world'. This mythical individual crossed Wyoming and reached Montana where he was stopped by the freezing winter. He built a small log cabin, settled himself in with his stores of

dried beans and firewood, kept one cow and let the rest of the herd go. In the spring, to his surprise, he found his animals in fairly good shape and realised that not only did the prairies of Montana stretch well over the horizon but that the grass was good and the land fertile.

Between 1918 and 1922, some 80,000 settlers arrived in the region and began to put up fencing round their property, as everyone in America had always done. But, within a few years, three-quarters of them had given up the idea of living there and left a land which they considered too far away from the other states, unfriendly and altogether too big. Those who stayed considered themselves real Westerners, whether they were smallholders or rich farmers with thousands of acres.

The small farmers now have a hard choice to make

between selling their land and keeping their traditional way of life, which is close to nature but so unprofitable that they are often obliged to take part-time jobs outside farming. Some corporations are very interested in Montana and Wyoming; the mining companies in particular buy up the land and start open-cast mining for copper, silver or even coal. The offers made by these companies are sometimes out of all proportion to the value of the land for farming, but many owners refuse stubbornly. They were born here, their fathers built the ranch house with pine logs cut from the local forest, they love their animals and this is where they intend to be buried.

Getting a little action

In view of the distances which separate not only the farms but also the towns, rodeos provide an opportunity for social contact and a chance to renew the community spirit by turning the skill of the cattlemen into an entertainment. From the beginning of spring until the end of summer, posters in all the shop windows announce the dates of these crucial events.

The exact programme is fixed well in advance. The day starts with a parade headed by the local high school band marching down the main street to get everyone in the mood and to introduce the riders mounted on their freshly groomed horses. The cowboys' red or blue neck-cloths float in the breeze, their boots and spurs gleam and they are seated on their heavy saddles of tooled leather. The whole parade moves straight down the street to the enclosure, which is surrounded by open stands for the jury and spectators. The events are announced over the loud-speaker and the judges give the official signal to begin.

The first event is some trick riding, which involves young men and women on horseback rushing into the ring and showing what they can do at full gallop. Slipping their feet out of the stirrups and holding onto the pommel of the saddle with both hands, they vault over the horse from side to side. The jury of local celebrities and former top riders awards the prizes. Then comes the turn of the 10- to 12-year-olds, who are already accomplished riders and working hard on their parents' farms in their spare time. They stand waiting, lasso in hand, facing the entrance gate to the arena. The instant it opens, a group of calves rushes in and the children surge forward – anyone who ties down a calf within the time limit can keep it. But the highlight of the rodeo is the bronco busting, which involves staying on the back of a young, untamed horse without a saddle or a bridle to hold on to. Even

Starting in Canyon Valley in the middle of Yellowstone Park, parties set off on horseback on trips lasting for several days. Official guides point out wildlife and keep their customers safe.

The first National Park to be created in the United States, Yellowstone remains the biggest. Its rivers and lakes are full of rainbow trout as well as many different kinds of salmon.

more difficult and much more dangerous is the steer riding. The enormous animal begins by spinning round and charging as soon as the cowboy leaps on its back. Whoever can stay on longest wins a silver belt buckle but most riders are pleased to stay in place for three or four seconds.

The Great American potato field

When they left the high plateaux of the Rockies, the early pioneers split up. Some travelled northwards into the unknown, while others turned south towards California and its golden promise. Those who stayed in the north either farmed the Snake River Plain, eventually turning it into the great American potato field, or wandered into the subdivision of the Rockies known as the Bitterroot Mountains, to develop some of the most productive silver mines in the United States in the Coeur d'Alene district, close to Idaho's border with Washington.

Idaho earned its nickname of 'the potato state' through the mechanised production of the mighty tuber. Nowadays over 4 million acres are irrigated by water pumped from the Snake River, with sugar beet being the other important root crop.

The silver mines of the north are still being worked after more than a century of production. Separated into over 20 different shafts, the area has yielded more than 2 billion dollars' worth of ore since operations began. However, the technological and engineering skill needed to achieve this has been considerable for the geological strata surrounding the ores are complex and far from easy to penetrate.

Coeur d'Alene is also known for another, somewhat less expected event – a Scottish Highland Festival. Every July the substantial number of Scots who still live in the state gather to celebrate their heritage with a brisk display of Highland dancing in their clan tartans – to the sound, of course, of the bagpipes.

Idaho was settled by Basque shepherds from the Franco-Spanish border and by Scots. Adrift in a foreign land, most people tried to keep the customs of their homelands alive and so, on the last frontiers of the west, songs and dances native to these parts of Europe still flourish.

Western Idaho is a green ocean rippling across gently curving hills. Off the beaten track, it has few tourists and is a region of small farms or very large agricultural enterprises. The high sand dunes in the south, and the wheat-filled valleys of the west are in sharp contrast to the mountains of the centre, which are still full of big game such as deer. In Clearwater, it has the largest forest of white pine in the world.

The enchantment of Oregon

The famous Oregon Trail is still rutted by the thousands of waggon wheels that followed the northern route across the Rocky Mountains to reach the forests where pioneers became farmers and trappers, big game hunters and fur traders. However, it was not simply that the states of the Pacific North-West were remote. Once the settlers had established themselves, they had to make a living – and trading with the rest of the United States was not easy. Until the Northern Pacific Railroad reached Portland, Oregon in 1883, the only way for large volumes of produce or manufactured goods to reach the main American markets was by ship round Cape Horn, still one of the most dangerous sea passages in the world. In 1893, Seattle was finally connected by the Great Northern Railway to the markets and exchanges of Chicago and the Mid-West. This enabled the logging industry to exploit the potential of the magnificent forests of the Pacific coast.

The traffic in fur that attracted many people to the region caused Oregon to be known as the beaver state. Now, with the trade long since dead, the state is a paradise for wildlife. The huge dark forests of Douglas fir, Sitka spruce and western hemlock in the national parks seem to stop only when they meet the waves of the Pacific Ocean. If you reach the coast as dusk is falling, a light salty mist veils the lines of sand dunes which separate the forest from the sea. Adventurous spirits can leave the highway and run down the sandy slopes to the cold waters to spot the baby seals before they swim away and clamber onto the safety of a spray-washed rock at the foot of a cliff.

With people living amid such natural pleasures, it is not surprising that 'green' issues made a big impact in the North-West before they affected the rest of America. For many years there have been laws

Harvesting wheat is an exact operation and the farmer must choose the optimum moment to start cutting. His livelihood depends on his judgement, so his calculations must be correct.

Frontiers are invisible on the prairies. When the grain is ripe, long lines of combine harvesters advance over the golden sea. Their synchronised advance not only looks spectacular, it is also the most efficient way of cutting a field in one sweep without leaving gaps on uneven terrain.

covering the recovery and recycling of glass bottles, and this explains why bottle bank bins are found outside the big stores and in all the town squares. Oregon was one of the first states in America to introduce a system in which its citizens could take the initiative, an example that has now been followed by many other states. This arrangement allows the citizens to put forward their own ideas for a new law, which is known as the 'initiative petition process'. The proposer then needs to collect the signatures of a fixed percentage of voters, usually 5 or 10 per cent, to have the proposal put onto the agenda of the legislature or put to the people in a referendum held at the same time as the next elections. By allowing the citizens to take the lead, the real concerns of the people can be given an airing in a way that is binding on the professional politicians if a majority say yes.

The green movement has also made itself felt in the shopping malls of the North-West where chains of vegetarian restaurants offering organically grown

food have opened. The initiative has come from those who, dissatisfied with their own lives and jobs, have set up ecological centres where the tables are decorated with bunches of wild flowers, nobody smokes and the customers tuck into honey cakes washed down by fruit juices or various herbal infusions. These restaurants are expanding at an amazing rate and threaten to oust the more traditional fast-food takeaways and snack-bars.

Another innovation created in Oregon has had a much more direct effect on homes throughout the world, although few people are aware of the origins of

their pleasure. At any large florists in a dozen countries, at any time of the year, there is a good chance that the stock will include lilies which were grown under glass in Holland. Their bold orange or yellow faces, plain or speckled, stare up at the would-be purchaser. A generation ago such lilies were unknown as cut flowers yet they are now sold worldwide. They are the result of the efforts of one man, Jan de Graaf, and the organisation he created, the Oregon Bulb Farms.

De Graaf was a man with a mission: he wanted to create a new lily that would be both beautiful and

tough. Many lilies were grown round the world but most were very vulnerable to viruses and therefore had little in the way of commercial prospects. He and his staff hybridised the most improbable combinations until they struck lucky and created the Mid-Century Hybrids, of which the bold orange variety known as 'Enchantment' is now a familiar sight in many homes. Oregon was chosen as the site for this experimental work because its climate is just right for growing lilies. Moist winds from the Pacific prevent the summers from getting too hot and the winters becoming too cold.

The good life

Recent national polls show that Americans consider Seattle, the biggest city in the North-West, to be the 'most liveable city' in America. Its citizens cannot decide whether to be flattered, or worried in case the description attracts more immigrants and makes the place less 'liveable'.

Perhaps Americans are so attracted to the city and the state of Washington because they can find 20th century amenities in an unspoilt landscape. For example, a monorail runs from the downtown area to the Seattle Center on a single track suspended above the road so that it does not interfere with the traffic. This allows the passengers to make the trip in two minutes. In the Center, which was the site of the World Fair of 1962, the Space Needle stands with its 607-foot tower topped by a revolving restaurant that resembles a flying saucer. A lift shaped like a miniature space shuttle shoots up to the bar/restaurant at the top. Patrons get a wonderful panorama of the entire city, the waters of Puget Sound, Lake Washington and the Olympic Mountains. They can admire the dense, untouched acres of forest without ever leaving the bar.

To the south, dominating the horizon, the Cascade Range is topped by the magnificent Mount Rainier, an extinct volcano crowned with eternal snows. Behind it stands another volcano, Mount St Helens, which Washingtonians no longer admire with any degree of calm. Until the spring of 1980, the citizens of Seattle

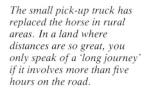

The small pick-up truck has replaced the horse in rural areas. In a land where distances are so great, you only speak of a 'long journey' if it involves more than five hours on the road.

The American sheriff did not die with the end of the pioneer days of the 19th century. In this country, where local democracy has gone so much farther than in Europe, he is the elected official in charge of law enforcement in small communities throughout the continent.

looked upon the area as a great place to spend the weekend if you liked the open air. Then, in March of that year, Mount St Helens returned from the dead to end a silence of 123 years. Weeks of minor earthquakes and grumbling eruptions shook the area, warning the police, vulcanologists and the local population that something was afoot. It gave the authorities plenty of time to clear the immediate area and enabled vulcanologists to set up their cameras and instruments to study this newly active volcano. Few of them expected what happened next.

On May 18, without any warning that something extraordinary was going to happen, another earthquake cracked open the entire north slope of the volcano. Like a bottle of malevolent champagne, the uncorked gases and liquid rock exploded through the gap with a force equivalent to 500 Hiroshima-sized atomic bombs. A column of ash and steam went straight up for 6 miles and one cubic mile of rock just disappeared. Two dozen lakes were erased from the face of the earth as an avalanche of boiling mud and rock scoured the landscape. Millions of mature trees were flattened like inconsequential splinters as a fireball of superheated gas and lava fragments scorched the earth, travelling at over 100 mph. The human toll reached 70, while more than 11 million fish perished in the instantaneous holocaust. Winds blew the ash to the east, leaving a 2-inch blanket on roads up to 260 miles away. Yet within a week spiders were spinning their webs across the debris of the ruptured forest. By the end of the summer, tree seedlings had appeared through the ash. On the fourth anniversary of the eruption, Douglas firs 4 feet high could be found in the shadow of Mount St Helens. Nature is clearly very resilient.

These riders are enjoying a traditional meal of pork and baked beans cooked over an open fire, washed down by a cup of coffee. Then tales are swapped about Big Foot, a legendary creature that is supposed to wander through the huge pine forests of Washington State.

This pioneers' cabin in Champoeg Park, Oregon, is quite large and luxurious compared to the majority of the old-time homes that had only two rooms – one used as a kitchen-living room and the other as a sleeping-place.

After crossing the Cascade Mountains south-east of Seattle, you come to a series of huge lakes fed by mountain streams. Boat trips carry tourists through a series of islands that are the remnants of extinct volcanoes, like this group on Lake Skaagit in Washington State.

The huge forests of aspens in Wyoming, Montana and Idaho create successive waves of changing colour throughout the year: a mosaic of reds, greens and yellows depending on the age of the trees. The trees grow very quickly and can reach a height of 60 feet. They can look very attractive in the garden for, thanks to their long, thin stems, aspen leaves tremble in the slightest breeze.

Skunks are not much bigger than cats, and can be found wherever there are forests. They can be tamed but this can be a risky business for the animal squirts out an evil-smelling fluid whenever it feels threatened.

The Pacific salmon has to run the gauntlet of fishermen working the open sea and those casting their nets further inshore, such as here in Puget Sound near Seattle. Most fishing permits in Washington State are issued to Indians, who have fought hard to keep their traditional rights.

The Alaskan brown bear lives in the more remote areas of Alaska. These omnivorous animals will eat almost anything – game, fish, berries and sometimes even grass.

A more benign face of nature comes from another direction. Whales often come up Puget Sound, the fine natural harbour opposite Seattle, to take shelter from storms at sea or merely because they have lost their way. In 1978 the local radio announced that a whale had been found in the Sound. This in itself was nothing special, but what roused public attention was the fact that a fisherman had rounded it up in a net and intended to sell it to an aquarium. Within hours the fishing boat was surrounded by an armada of aggrieved citizens in motorboats, yachts and canoes. Nearly everyone in Seattle has some kind of water transport and they had appeared spontaneously to insist on the whale's release. In the face of this unprecedented demonstration of mammalian solidarity the coastal authorities had little alternative but to order the fisherman to let the animal go, and the small grampus whale was able to swim out to sea to rejoin its pod in the ocean.

The North Cascade Highway leads to the interior of Washington State. A billboard by the side of the mountainous route is painted with an enormous black foot on a yellow background announcing that this is the country of 'Big Foot', a sort of American Abominable Snowman that the newspapers and television feature regularly. Unlike the coast, with its mild climate and thick vegetation, the interior, caught in the rainshadow of the mountains, is arid and short of water. It took all the ingenuity of 20th-century engineering to create the irrigation systems which led to the development of the apple orchards which now flourish on the plateau.

Of course, Washington is not just scenery. The Boeing aircraft company has been the mainstay of the local economy since the 1920s, although the number of its employees has tended to fluctuate wildly according to whether it has secured the latest defence contract or not. This is the place where the jumbo jet was conceived and manufactured, and where they continue to roll off the production line. The port, with over 50 miles of wharves, is a major terminal for container traffic and has benefited enormously from America's reorientation towards the Pacific Basin and Japan. It is also the exit point for much of the region's timber.

The coastline additionally harbours something a little more sinister. The United States Navy is busy building the base for its next generation of nuclear submarines at Kitsap County on Puget Sound. One of the largest military construction projects in American history, its cost and that of the Trident missile system is so vast that even the Americans can only afford to build ten submarines to deliver the weapon.

High hopes and high wages

In the Aleut language, *alashka* means 'big land'. In 1966, seven years after Alaska had become the 49th state featured on the Stars and Stripes, the United States Government discovered that although the state was big, it might not be big enough. The representatives of Aleuts, Indians and Innuit, the people who used to be known as Eskimos, filed claims with the federal government for rights to most of Alaska's 375 million acres.

It took several years before the American Congress agreed on legislation to settle the claims. This worked

In Alaska, fishing and hunting are not merely pastimes but an essential source of food. Children learn how to use a gun at a very early age.

Fishing is one of the traditional occupations of the Innuit. In winter they cut holes in the ice and lower a line into the water beneath. This eskimo examines his catch in the snow.

to the advantage of the native people, who knew that Alaskan oil was needed and that construction of the pipeline could not proceed until a bill was passed. This leverage was instrumental in the passage of the Alaska Native Claims Settlement Act in 1971.

This legislation awarded 40 million acres to the 53,000 native people who lived in the state, as well as a cash settlement of 1000 million dollars. The award of land was more than the total previously awarded to all the remainder of the country's native people, while the money was four times the sum distributed by the US Indian Claims Commission since it was founded in 1946. This victory was made possible to a large extent by the discovery of oil in Prudhoe Bay on Alaska's northern shore in 1968 by Atlantic Richfield and Humble Oil.

The discovery of so much potential profit in such an inaccessible spot created problems for the oil companies that they had never had to face before. Drilling the wells in such conditions had been difficult enough, but solving the problem of how to move the crude oil to the refineries was even more taxing. Sea ice made the construction of a port on the north shore impractical. In the end, an 800-mile pipeline to the port of Valdez on the southern shore in Prince William Sound proved to be the best solution. A consortium was formed to build the pipeline, 100 million dollars' worth of pipe was delivered and a construction schedule was agreed. Then they had to wait, first until the claims of the native peoples were satisfied and then until the environmental objections were overcome. Only in 1974 did work start. Three years and 8 billion dollars later, the most expensive construction project in American history was finished and the oil could flow.

To service the well heads in Prudhoe Bay, the oil companies have built 'anti-Arctic accommodation' for

A new race of pioneers has turned to Alaska as an escape from the rat race of commercial life. Mostly from California, many of these pioneers build saunas, heated by wood-burning stoves, alongside their cabins so that they can take a hot steam bath. They can then run down the log jetty and plunge into the icy waters, like native Scandinavians.

their employees, to help fight the strains and stresses of loneliness. Inside these glass and concrete constructions, the companies have tried to recreate the American way of life. After spending 12 hours staring at precision instruments, controlling the pressure in the pipeline or patrolling among snow-covered or ice-encrusted pipes, the technicians can find real aspens grown in hothouses that are ready to drop their leaves when the thermostat creates autumnal conditions. They can swim in the heated pool, eat their favourite food, go to the recreation rooms or the cinema and then back to their rooms, furnished exactly like any to be found in an American motel. Once the seven-day stint is over, they leave their workplace and go off at the company's expense to spend a week in Fairbanks or Anchorage, the two biggest towns in Alaska, which

To compensate for the appalling conditions, the oil companies pay very high wages to the technicians and maintenance teams working on the 800-mile Alaskan pipeline. This means that many of them can afford to buy a plane in which to get away during breaks.

Fur auctions are carried out extremely quickly. A good auctioneer will spice his announcements with a witty running commentary that amuses the buyers and improves the sales figures. The trappers are licensed by the state to bring in their quota of reindeer, caribou, fox, brown bear, wolf and seal skins.

between them account for nearly half the population.

It is as if the oil companies have done their best to ensure that their engineers and technicians who have to live in Alaska know as little of it as possible. What, unless they break away from the routine, do these outsiders know of the strange world of 24-hour sunlight in the summer and months of gloom in the winter? Most of the land is covered by the low-grade conifer forest known as taiga, while the subsoil is permanently frozen, in places down to 1300 feet. Only the topsoil thaws in the summer, perhaps to a depth of 3 feet. The best prospects for Alaska's economic growth seem to be more mineral discoveries and the development of the tourist industry.

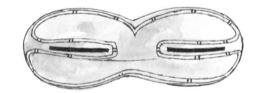

The Innuit have not been deported to unfamiliar regions as have other American native peoples because they fought for their cause with great political skill. They now have the choice of maintaining their traditional way of life or adapting to the modern world.

Out of the 500,000 inhabitants of the state of Alaska, about 10 per cent are native people. Although they have adopted various modern inventions such as prefabricated houses and snowmobiles, many of them continue to use traditional objects like the carved bone sun-glasses with narrow slits or the thick, fur-lined boots which are worn for most of the day.

The Mid-West

From Oklahoma to North Dakota, Minnesota to Mississippi, the great plains are the heart of the United States. It was here that modern America was forged in the bond between the agricultural output of the prairies and the industrial output of the north and east during the 19th century. It was on these plains that the nation overcame its colonial past and the railways carried it towards the future. Amid the oceans of golden wheat and green maize, the visitor stands not only at the crossroads of American history, but at the very core of the land of the immigrants.

The Mid-West is a land of big farms and small towns; a land of conservative values that lead to radical politics; a land that voted for Ronald Reagan only to discover that less government meant a cut in farm subsidies. However, on its northern rim a number of major cities cling to the shorelines of the Great Lakes that are the antithesis of the agricultural idyll. The steel foundries of Chicago and the production lines of Detroit are no one's idea of fun city. But without these scars on the landscape, the golden fields would be a heart without a beat.

The Mid-West is also a land of monotonous vistas, broken only occasionally by a few trees. The land is flat, cut up into uniform rectangles – dark red, bright green, golden yellow or deepest black, depending on the time of year. These rich plains provide the farmers with fertile soil, but initially it was packed so hard that a blacksmith, John Deere, had to invent the steel plough back in 1837 before it could be opened up and sown with the cereals that have made its fortune.

Nowhere in America are eyes lifted so often to the sky which brings the rain to swell the grain in summer. But the sky carries a two-edged sword that can hang

Railways helped to turn America into the industrial giant it is today. The system now concentrates on transporting freight because airlines have taken over the job of carrying the people across the continent. But elderly hobos still 'jump the tracks' for a free ride as they have for decades.

like the blade of Damocles over the harvest. The wind, hail and tornadoes which hurl themselves down this enormous corridor can sweep over the plains and reduce the country to desolation in a few hours.

If you go into Minden, or any of a hundred small towns in Nebraska, and ask if the hot winds are always so strong in July, someone will probably reply that they are nothing out of the ordinary and that you should only begin to worry if you hear a warning siren. Local people take a morbid delight in pinning up photos of the tornadoes that have passed through the town. In the prints the ferocious winds seemed to be picking at the plain like so many black fingers reaching down from the sky, the cylindrical shapes cutting swathes of destruction through the land. The farmers, mostly staunch Protestants, compare these disasters to the plagues of Egypt in the Bible.

The plainsman can see the narrow black cloud coming over the distant horizon with its top whirling upwards, filling the sky and advancing slowly as if towards some mysterious destination. The sirens sound the warning and everyone goes down into the cellars to wait until this oversized suction cleaner has passed, whirling around its epicentre at more than 300 miles an hour.

The modern Indian trading post is no log cabin in the forest, and this wayside store acts as an agency for the people who live on the local reservation.

An eye on the prize

The most important event of the year after Christmas, say the farmers, is the State Fair. These annual agricultural gatherings take place in every prairie state between June and October, the most famous being the Iowa State Fair at Des Moines. Held at the end of August, this fair lasts for six days and attracts visitors from the entire region. People from the neighbouring states come and camp around the fairground. Caravans in a variety of shapes and sizes appear, bringing animals, patchwork, jams and preserves to be entered in open contests.

Under huge, covered sheds, specially built to hold the various groups of combatants, every aspect of farming life is represented and everything is subject to fierce scrutiny: bread and cakes, animals, arts and crafts and needlework. In addition, every afternoon at two there are horseshoe-throwing competitions. Two short stakes are set up, a few yards apart. Each player takes his turn, standing beside one stake armed with three horseshoes. The horseshoe has to be thrown so that it lands round the opposite stake. Distances between stake and horseshoes are measured and points calculated before doing the same thing in the

opposite direction. The competition is fierce as this is one of the most prestigious events of the fair.

Children also play a special part in the general activity. Most of them belong to the Young Farmers Club of America, which means they can start learning at an early age. Throughout the year they take part in organised outings, follow nature trails, and have their own exhibits and contests at the State Fairs.

In one of the tents, reserved for arts and crafts, the canvases reveal the painters' love for the plains. There are pictures of windmills which pump the water from artesian wells for the fields and animals, sunsets over endless fields of golden corn, and dark whirlwinds threatening the horizon. Others express themselves by creating patchwork with intricate patterns, or finely crocheted lace.

In every fair there is always a trade exhibition featuring the latest essential chemicals, the biggest and best tractors, and the most sophisticated farming machinery manufactured in Chicago or Detroit. Confronted by these monsters of efficiency, the farmers wear much the same glazed expressions as the Indians might have worn when they saw the first Spanish horses. And just as the horse transformed the life of the Plains Indians, farming machinery has transformed the lives of those who now inhabit the prairies. Yet fewer and fewer farmers are rich enough to buy these expensive machines, built to cope with thousands of acres. Unless they commit themselves to a purchase, however, the small farmers will be unable to compete with the big corporations that control vast sections of these territories through their agents. It is a situation that has forced many farmers off the land to work in the big cities and their absence is beginning to be felt in the small communities, which are slowly dying despite their determination to persist.

During the 1980s, when produce prices fell along with land values, the independent farmer became an endangered species. Only big companies had the financial resources to sit out the agricultural depression until good times returned.

Sophisticated irrigation systems are necessary to make the drylands of the Mid-West productive and bind the soil. Tornadoes sweep this land every year and in May 1934 the wind carried away 350 million tons of topsoil from the Dakotas and dumped it in the Atlantic.

Meet me in St Louis

The two greatest rivers in North America flow through the Mid-West from one end to the other. The Mississippi and the Missouri merge just north of St Louis, one coming from northern Minnesota, the other from northern Montana, both wandering lazily through prairies and plains before passing the stainless steel arch that marks the gateway to the West.

Most towns in the Mid-West were built on rivers because water provided the only means of transport until the railways arrived. The famous paddle-steamers of the Mississippi carried people, animals and merchandise, and it was by river that the pioneers were able to reach the foothills of the Rockies and find the only two useable crossings. For half a century these great rivers were the link between, on the one hand the established townships of the East Coast and,

The era of big farming requires very careful accountancy and a constant awareness of government regulations.

Before the Europeans arrived, the indigenous people only knew one cereal: maize, also known in America as corn. The Indians taught the newcomers how to grow this crop and now the United States exports three-quarters of all the maize grown in the world.

In this featureless landscape, the only landmarks are farm buildings like this barn. Walls are wooden and the roof is tin sheeting. Water has to be drawn from a well and the windmill pumps it up.

The most productive arable land in America is in Iowa and it raises 10 per cent of all the cereals grown in the United States. In order to maximise their profits, some farmers have formed co-operatives while others have amalgamated to form large agricultural companies.

on the other, the South and the immigrants, pioneers and adventurers in search of gold who were drawn to the new frontiers.

Nowadays canals have tamed the rivers, taking the extra water that scoured the shallows; but in the beginning it was very different and the boats could only get under way when they had a qualified pilot on board who knew the channels. The Missouri is called the 'great muddy' on account of the vast quantities of sediment it carries, and it was the changing deposition of these sediments that caused the difficulties. The flat-bottomed paddle-steamers were designed to surmount these problems. Vessels had to negotiate sandbanks which shifted from one season to the next, or perhaps fallen trees that had stuck in places where the water was unexpectedly deep and were invisible from the surface, so the amount of water that the boat drew was critical. Some of these old paddle-steamers, like the *Sergeant Floyd*, are still operating, though nowadays oil has replaced the old coal-burning boilers.

Many American legends, handed down by word of mouth, are based on stories about the Mississippi and the Missouri. They were also the basis of some of the work of one of America's greatest writers. Mark Twain was born in Hannibal, a small town on the Missouri, and became a river pilot, basing *The Adventures of Tom Sawyer* and *The Adventures of Huckleberry Finn* on his own experiences. He took his pen name from the cry of the leadsman testing the depth of the water, who shouted 'mark twain', meaning it was two fathoms deep at that point. Every summer the small town of Hannibal relives the works of its most famous son by acting out a passage from one of his books. Groups of children can be seen proudly painting the white fences round their gardens, imitating Tom Sawyer who before setting out on his adventures was told by his aunt to repaint her fence.

Detroit still dominates the American automobile industry, and many Mid-Westerners are employed making cars, tractors, harvesters and vehicles of all kinds. But the factories of the South, frequently owned by the Japanese, are starting to make their presence felt.

Social life in small towns has developed to compensate for the feeling of isolation in the middle of the plains. Even in get-up-and-go America, sitting and chatting in front of the local store would never be stigmatised as laziness.

Truck drivers have replaced cowboys in American mythology as a symbol of freedom. Their customised cabs and life on the open road appeal to the imagination of suburban America.

These racing tractors, like stock-cars, have been modified to increase their performance on the track. They are one more manifestation of the American desire to turn any skill into a competition.

At the end of summer and in early autumn most villages organise a local fair, an opportunity to see the latest farming machinery and to show off the best of the recent harvest.

From the earliest age children are encouraged to take part in farming activities. They are given a calf, a lamb or a piglet, and made completely responsible for its care. In this way they become part of the family enterprise and quickly learn the disciplines of keeping livestock.

In the modern Mid-West, the chickens may provide the eggs but it's the computer that creates the profits. Despite its idyllic image, farming has always involved long hours of hard work under conditions that are often very trying.

The Lord's platter

The Mid-West is firmly embedded in the Bible Belt and its small towns frequently contain more churches than bars or petrol stations. The region is overwhelmingly Protestant although there are many different sects, so the various churches or temples carry the names of their faiths above the entrance. The buildings are merely enlarged houses or square white constructions with painted bell-towers and the interiors are as simple as the chapel's silhouette.

Whether in Hastings, Nebraska, or Terre Haute, Indiana, the different sects are much given to organising evening parties known as 'church dinners' – meals held in the big meeting place in the church basement. In spring and summer they provide a social occasion for the isolated families who sometimes find the solitude of the great plains something of a strain. Traditionally the women cook at home, each preparing their favourite recipes before spending an entire afternoon turning the big room into a community cafeteria. These dinners provide an excuse for changing out of blue overalls and into their 'best bib and tucker'. The latest news can be exchanged or farming problems discussed over fried chicken and corn on the cob. Everyone makes a small financial contribution which will go towards the church or some favourite charity supported by the wives. When the meal is over the women wash up and tidy the hall while the men carry on talking or start up a game of horseshoes. In summer everyone wanders outside into the night. The warm air is stirred by a light breeze smelling of honeysuckle while hundreds of fireflies dance a silent ballet down the darkening streets and over the fields.

In contrast with the flat plains of Kansas, Nebraska and Iowa, the northern states bordering the Great Lakes *possess forest-covered hills which give a glorious autumn display.*

Reinventing the past

The 630-foot high stainless steel rainbow known as the Gateway Arch, which was finished in 1966 and stands beside the Mississippi in downtown St Louis, is the most distinctive landmark in the Mid-West. It commemorates the starting point of the immigrants, mainly from Germany, Ireland and Scandinavia who, filled with the hope of finding a better life, bought their waggons in St Louis before setting out for the West.

The city was founded in 1764 as one of the chain of French trading posts that extended down the Mississippi Valley. But another 70 years passed before the city was redesigned and the authorities began to lay it out in its present form. St Louis really started to prosper after the end of the Civil War as America overhauled Europe in a massive economic spurt that took it to number one in so many of the world's industrial league tables. The city was at the crossroads of America, and as the country grew, so did St Louis.

The farmers of the Mid-West are as concerned about the quality of their herds as any other farmer and are quick to take the opportunity offered by the local State Fair to demonstrate their achievements in their livestock breeding programmes.

In 1904, the city became the venue of the World Fair. Such events always leave reminders behind them. In this case, St Louis was left with Forest Park, a green lung in the centre of the city.

St Louis stood like a beacon on the plains because it was the only metropolis for hundreds of miles. Most farmers only had the opportunity to visit the nearest small town which looked much the same as every other small town that dotted the landscape: a main street with a post office, a bank, a church, a drug-store, a hotel, the sheriff's·office and a gaol. Nobody lived there permanently except the owners of these establishments. The odd traveller passed through from time to time.

Hollywood has a lot to answer for in the image that it has created of 19th-century rural America. From a motley crowd of petty criminals, the occasional psychopath and a sprinkling of prostitutes who in-habited a few isolated townships, it has created a mythology that has endured far longer than the original denizens of the West ever lived. In nourishing its need for movement, action and a simplified morality, it has fostered an illusion that orchestrated violence was the decisive element in society and has obscured the real heroes of the plains: the men and women who endured the ferocious summers and the bitter winters long before anyone invented the air conditioning unit. It was these immigrants who wrung modern America from the dust of the plains.

Ironically, in an attempt to attract tourists and so bolster their flagging economies as their citizens have slowly leaked away to the big cities, various small towns across the Mid-West have tried to revive the excitements of the 'good old days'. Dodge City has built a long main street reproducing the traditional lay-out and every July steps back 100 years as the former 'queen of the cowboy towns' relives its illu-sions of grandeur. Young men dressed as sheriffs complete with gun holsters and a badge of office hand out slips 'condemning you to a prison meal' – in reality a free meal in their restaurant. Another offers 'a night in the caboose', meaning a free pass to their

saloon-bar whose swinging doors welcome all comers throughout the week.

The small town of Lafayette, set in the low hills of Indiana, goes in for a slightly different charade every August when a village of Indian tepees puts in an appearance. This is supplemented by all kinds of tents and caravans which mingle during a week-long celebration called 'pioneer days', in which most locals wear traditional Mid-West outfits or the national costume of their country of origin or dress according to their religion.

A young man in a sandy-coloured leather shirt and trousers decorated with long fringes is sitting outside one tepee. A French tricolour flutters above his head as he sharpens an axe. He is a descendant of one of the 18th-century trappers who travelled the Mid-West before the Americans bought the territory from France in 1803. His ears prick up as an announcement is made in the distance. He flicks his thumb across his blade one last time before striding off to compete in the axe-throwing competition.

Local fairs are often the occasion for some grotesque contests. These children are competing to see how many watermelon segments they can eat before they are bloated to capacity.

All change in Chicago

Although the people of the plains love reliving the rural myths of the their past, the Mid-West is also home to some of the greatest industrial complexes in the world. Detroit is, of course, the headquarters of the American motor industry and the capital of the three great empires of Ford, General Motors and Chrysler. This was where Henry Ford, himself the son of a farmer, reinvented the system of mass production first pioneered by the Chinese centuries before in their porcelain factories. Even Ford, who was alleged to have said 'History is bunk', was bitten by the bug when he had the idea of setting up or reconstituting buildings marking outstanding moments of American history in a section of his Open Air Museum 10 miles from Detroit in Greenfield Village. More than 100 buildings have now been assembled: slave cabins, the courthouse where Lincoln practised, Thomas Edison's laboratory, various small specialist shops and even a Dutch windmill.

Detroit's chemical industry is less well-known than its car producers but it is still important, particularly for the farmers of the plains who have become dependent on its fertilisers and pesticides. Most of the plants, which draw on the huge deposits of salt that underlie Detroit, are located on the outskirts of the city, beyond Ford's enormous complex at Rouge.

However, even Detroit is dwarfed by Chicago, the core of which spreads along 29 miles of the carefully groomed shore of Lake Michigan. But this is only the

Even today, wooden houses dominate the countryside and the suburbs of America. This material is always less expensive than brick, which is only used for city housing to avoid the fire risk.

centre of the city which, because of its energetic growth, is spreading and merging with its neighbours, like Gary to the south-east. Chicago remains so vigorous because a web of industries contributes to its economy; it is not dominated by one sector, like Detroit. If American car sales flag, as they have in the 1980s, the city of Detroit is in trouble. When Chicago's furniture industry hit hard times, the steel industry was there to pick up the pieces.

Like several other cities of the interior, Detroit started out as a French trading post. This quest for furs, primarily beaver, all started when the French king began wearing a beaver hat. The French aristocracy immediately followed suit and a new fashion was born – one that opened up a continent.

The rather waterlogged site of Chicago at the southern end of Lake Michigan was not thought to be a good one but its convenience overcame all the objections. During the first half of the 19th century, the port became one of the major immigration routes into the plains. Then, in just a few years, Chicago's prospects were transformed when in 1848 a canal was cut that linked Lake Michigan with the Mississippi. This was followed by the arrival of the railway from New York in 1852. With the completion of the rail connection to the West Coast in 1869, the city's future looked assured.

But on October 8, 1871 Chicago was burned to the

The small village of Custer was established at the time of the Indian wars and named in honour of the general who was killed at the Battle of Little Big Horn in 1876.

ground. Fanned by a furious wind from the south-west, a huge conflagration reduced all the wooden buildings to ashes in just over 24 hours. The heat was so intense that the underground water pipes melted. But Chicago's advantages were so great that it just bounced back, although this time the city fathers made sure that the architects worked in stone. The buildings that were created had a profound effect, not just on Chicago but on all 20th-century cities. It was in Chicago, not New York, that the skyscraper was invented. It was in the suburbs of Chicago that the architect Frank Lloyd Wright changed the design of the modern home. To this day, interest in these houses is so great that Oak Park, the suburb where most of them were built, contains a tour centre whose sole purpose is to organise visits to the Wright homes.

Chicago today is still growing. The city's main industry is steel, followed by the manufacture of machinery, particularly electrical equipment. Yet the food industry remains important, although the infamous stockyards and abattoirs have been moved to accommodate redevelopments so that Omaha and Sioux City have taken over the killing pens. Chicago's pivotal position in North America has ensured that its role in the nation's transport system is still central and O'Hare Airport is the busiest in the world.

The city has also been very fortunate in its management team for it has avoided the mistakes that have

A canoe trip on a lake, an evening round the fire and nights spent under canvas are popular outings in Minnesota. The traditional Indian canoe is meant to be paddled from the kneeling position, which can be painful for the inexperienced.

When most of the best land had been settled by Europeans, the government created huge Indian reserves in the South, Mid-West and North-West, especially in the states of Oklahoma and South Dakota. These young Apaches live in one of the reserves of South Dakota.

wrecked so many American cities. Detroit, for example, allowed its central area to become run down as those who were affluent enough migrated to the suburbs in the 1950s. The city council then made the matter much worse by investing large amounts of capital in miles of freeways that would keep the cars moving between the suburbs, but isolating the centre. Only in the late 1960s did the dangers of the situation become apparent, when the citizens who had been left behind exacted their revenge and took a torch to the city. For a few days, Americans watched helpless in the face of urban insurrection as the rioters shot it out with the police. Only then did the country realise that something needed to be done.

Chicago never took this road. Its beaches were kept clean, the parks were maintained and, where other cities allowed old buildings to be demolished and the sites used as parking lots, Chicago created pedestrian piazzas and a new generation of skyscrapers. In these new public spaces, what is probably the greatest collection of 20th-century street sculpture was installed with pieces by many of the world's most famous artists, including a Picasso and a witty 100-foot high baseball bat by Claes Oldenburg.

If the religious plainsman casts a wary eye on the bustle of Chicago, he might see a source of corruption, like the coastal cities of the East and West, which contradict the traditional American way of life. Milwaukee in Wisconsin, on the other hand, is often quoted as the model city. Its 700,000 inhabitants, mostly of German, Polish or Italian origin, are believed to practise the 'American dream', or at least the puritan's version of it: living together in a community which takes its responsibilities seriously, governs itself according to the laws of honesty and for whom hard work brings its own reward.

Of course, Germany is not merely the home of the upright citizen, it is also the home of the Bierkeller. It comes as no surprise, therefore, to discover that Milwaukee is a centre of American brewing and that there is a brewery right in the centre of town. Until the end of the 19th century such accomplishments were celebrated only locally, because of the distances involved in distributing any product in the United States and the changes in temperature that the beer would encounter on its route during the course of a year. But not only did the refrigerated railway waggon connect the Californian horticulturalists to a new market, it also worked wonders for the Milwaukee brewers, who could guarantee the quality of their product when it reached its destination.

The 630-foot high Gateway Arch was built on the banks of the Mississippi in St Louis to commemorate the pioneers of the 19th century who settled the plains. The city was always considered to be the gateway to the West because this was where the pioneers fitted themselves out, buying waggons, cattle, horses and tools, as well as hiring experienced guides to help them reach their goal.

Hallelujah!

On the way out of Milwaukee, a line of parked cars appears at the roadside in the middle of nowhere, while the owners can be seen following a path winding through the trees and bushes nearby. Soon the sounds of an accordion, clarinet and tuba fill the night air. The path finally opens up into a field where a small crowd is dancing polkas and waltzes around a bandstand. In the centre, an orchestra in Bavarian costume is paying homage to the genius of the Strauss family. This improvised beer garden is obviously a family affair: two small girls are dancing together; an elderly couple holding each other at arms' length rotate with obvious enjoyment; threesomes are practising the latest dance steps. The entertainment, which is held every Friday evening during the summer, includes a barbecue offering Polish or Bavarian sausages, served with sauerkraut on the side, washed down by cans of cold beer or Coca-Cola. The young people who are not interested in dancing have started up a game of baseball in a neighbouring field. This is not, however, just a social occasion but the prelude to something more spiritual.

Religious gatherings and revival meetings are very much part of life on the prairies and in the small towns. This means that men and some women evangelists travel from place to place urging a revival of the Christian faith and addressing the people freely and directly, Bible in hand, urging them to escape from the forces of evil and return to the 'true path'; these sessions can be either pure improvisations or elaborately staged. This is why these people have come together tonight: to return to their roots.

The best known of these itinerant preachers is undoubtedly Billy Graham, whose meetings have been televised and always attract huge crowds wherever he goes in the world. The biggest hall available will be hired and filled to bursting for four days by crowds coming to hear the 'good word'. While the seats are filling up, a choir 500 strong, dressed in white, arranged in a semi-circle around a small black rostrum, sings psalms and hymns. Suspended from the ceiling, an immense banner proclaims the words of Christ in scarlet letters: 'I am the Way, I am the Truth'. Between the rostrum and the choir, six men and women sit facing the audience. When the hall is full and a few evangelists have made the rounds to check that everything is in order, making sure the sound equipment is working and everyone is sitting comfortably, a certain air of expectancy, or even a touch of impatience begins to make itself felt.

At last, one of the six rises and goes to the microphone, discussing the latest happenings in town and making a few personal comments before concluding by emphasising the personal benefits that 'following the Way' has had on them. After the speaker is seated again, a second member of the six rises, addressing the audience as 'brothers and sisters' and confronting them with questions: Who among us

Sandwiched between the United States and Canada, the Great Lakes are so vast that they seem more like an inland sea. Farming and industrial products are shipped down the St Lawrence Seaway, which connects all the lakes, through a series of canals, to the Atlantic.

has never been tempted by the spirit of evil? Who among us has never failed in charity and honesty? Who among us has never wanted to commit adultery? Questions and speakers follow each other. Replies are shouted from every corner. The temperature is rising.

Suddenly a tall man in a dark suit crosses the platform and climbs up onto the rostrum. He glances calmly round the entire assembly and lays his Bible down in front of him. Absolute silence follows and the air of expectancy reaches its highest pitch. In a low voice, Billy Graham begins to speak. Everyday events suddenly become transcripts from the Bible, everyone's hopes and fears are described for everyone to hear, and everyone feels involved. In the name of all present, before God, on behalf of the whole nation, the preacher sets the example: he bows his head and humbly invites the assembly to come back to the 'path traced by God', so that 'the Way' may be followed by everyone. The choir breaks into an anthem while a collection is taken up to enable the audience to demonstrate the depth of its charitable feelings and to lead everybody to the good life. The enthusiasm increases with the singing; people leave their seats to join the choir and the disabled come forward on crutches or in wheelchairs to receive a special blessing from the evangelist.

Chicago built the first skyscraper in 1883 and still has the world's tallest, the Sears Building. Its streets and city centre have been maintained in a way that is an example to America's other major cities. Still at the centre of America's transportation system, the city's O'Hare Airport is reputed to be the busiest in the world, despite Los Angeles taking over as America's second-biggest city after New York.

The huge plate glass windows of the Hyatt Regency Hotel in the centre of Chicago help its profusion of plants and shrubs to create an elegant setting for diners. It is not far from the Art Institute and its magnificent collection of French painting.

Revival meetings are not always as big as this. Some say that the only 'true' ones are those held in the small chapels and that the 'true' evangelists preach to small congregations.

Another kind of gathering is held periodically in the small town of Beanblossom, Indiana, after the harvest. You will only find out about it if you are there at the right time. A banner across the main street proclaims 'Beanblossom's Old Settlers' Reunion'. All the oldest immigrants and their children wear badges announcing the year of their arrival. On this occasion, many families keep open house and everyone is welcome to come in for a chat and to enjoy a piece of apple or pumpkin pie. In the street, the children have set up stalls where they sell glasses of lemonade to earn some pocket money. There is even a greasy pole at the crossroads which anyone is welcome to climb in order to grab the 10 dollar bill fixed to the top.

The primary school has hired the local hall for an

Children buy pumpkins at Halloween and carve and paint them as ghoulish masks. At dusk on October 31 they go from house to house in their neighbourhood, dressed up as ghosts, witches or grinning monsters. Their challenge is 'trick or treat' for which they expect to be given sweets so that they will not play a trick on the owner.

The back alleys of Chicago, festooned with iron fire escapes, lack the glamour of the facades of the large hotels and skyscrapers.

These twin, circular apartment blocks use the lower storeys as a high-rise car park for the residents, who live on the floors above. Because Chicago has an efficient public transport system, the city's parking problems are not as acute as those of many other large American cities.

evening of square dancing. Couples line up and go through various intricate steps following the orders of the 'caller', who adds jokes and personal remarks to the announcements of the different figures, contributing much to the general entertainment. A few umbrellas set up in a nearby garden mean that at dusk everyone will gather there to listen to the music created by banjos, guitars and violins. Perhaps the enjoyment of these simple pleasures does indicate that the spirit of the immigrants is still alive and well after all.

Such 'down home' entertainments would have been much to the taste of Abraham Lincoln who, although he was born in Kentucky and grew up in Indiana, spent most of his adult life in Illinois travelling the state as a 'prairie lawyer'. Lincoln had little formal education but he taught himself the rudiments of grammar and mathematics. His dislike of farming led him to try a variety of jobs and while he was a storekeeper, legend has it that he walked three miles to return 20 cents change to a customer.

Lincoln took up law and passed his bar examination in 1836. Through hard work and much travelling he was soon earning more than the state governor. Politics took his fancy and he sat in the state legislature for six years. But it was only in the political upheavals that preceded the Civil War that his career suddenly turned towards the heights of the Presidency. His steadfast leadership during his country's greatest crisis set an example that is revered to this day.

The lifestyle of the plains Indians was perfectly adapted to their environment in which the enormous herds of bison played a dominant role. The animals furnished their hunters with meat, leather and thread for food, clothing and shelter.

When the first covered waggons rolled over the plains of the Mid-West the new farmers found the ground too hard for their ploughs. They had to wait for John Deere's steel blade, invented in 1837, in order to cut furrows in ground that had been pounded for centuries by the hooves of millions of bison.

Down South

The flavour of the South is as recognisable as a piece of pecan pie at a tasting contest – at least it used to be. Nowadays the South is on the move and the old traditions are being diluted as large numbers of newcomers migrate to thriving cities like Houston and Atlanta.

Perhaps the South was always a bit of an illusion. The gracious lifestyle and big houses with white pillars, which formed such a charming backdrop in *Gone with the Wind*, were supported by grinding poverty for both black and white tenants, subsistence farming, absentee landlords, widespread illiteracy and, in some places, racial brutality on a shocking scale.

Fortunately something has changed in the deep South, something that has destroyed forever the old illusions and the old reality. This new start may well be symbolised by a gun-toting black sheriff but its substance is found in the fields and factories that have changed the work and the wages of the people and raised their expectations and their pride. No longer are they bent over cotton bushes filling sacks. These days they drive giant mechanical pickers with air-conditioned cabs. That is, if they even grow cotton any more.

The divisions between the various regions in the United States are normally a little blurred at the edges but everyone knows where the South begins. Between 1765 and 1768 two Englishmen, Jeremiah Dixon and Charles Mason, surveyed the line of demarcation between Pennsylvania and Maryland for the Penn and Baltimore families to end the property disputes between them. The line at 39°43', which separates the Northern from the Southern states, became known as the Mason-Dixon Line, and the states to the south were called the land of Dixie. Washington is just south of that demarcation line.

Unable to settle on a site for the federal capital that would please everyone, the congressional representatives left it to George Washington to make the choice in 1790. He picked what seemed to him to be a neutral position, a virtually uninhabited area on the banks of the Potomac River which was easily accessible to both

During the last century hundreds of flat-bottomed paddle steamers travelled up and down the 2348 miles of the Mississippi. The coming of the railways and then the airlines decimated their numbers but some of these floating palaces still survive and carry tourists from New Orleans to St Louis.

the Northern and Southern states, could be reached by ocean-going vessels, but was not vulnerable to a surprise attack from the sea. It was also conveniently close to his home.

Once the city was off the drawing board, the District of Columbia was created with a special form of administration so that it would not be beholden to any individual state; but in the end the system proved to have unfortunate consequences. Although the city's population is 75 per cent black, Washington was run by a committee dominated by Southern senators. The consequence was that while fine speeches about equality were being made up on Capitol Hill by the nation's leaders, the city around them was the last to be desegregated. Only when the city achieved self-government in 1973 were the remaining traces of racial dominance removed.

Here at the end of April, the air is warm but not yet heavy with the oppressively humid atmosphere that blows in from the south and suffocates the capital during the summer. It is a lovely day and the city is at its best to receive visitors. As always, thousands of tourists are in town to see the sights, taking their guided tours around the Library of Congress or posing for snaps on the steps of the Capitol. Only the squirrels seem more numerous. Down towards the

Potomac, the Tidal Basin is enveloped in the exquisite pink of the flowering cherries which were given to the capital by the Japanese government in the 1920s.

Washington, always known to its citizens as 'DC', is not just a haven for politicians, tourists and television reporters. Through its 300,000 civil servants, it administers the affairs of the nation. Most of these workers live outside the capital in the 'burbs' of Virginia and Maryland. Every morning and evening they flood in and out like a mechanical tide, leaving their empty vehicles beached in the many parking lots scattered around town. Many people share the journey in a highly organised series of 'car pools' in order to commute between downtown and the suburban shopping centres that circle the city. It is in these outer car parks that the commuters leave their own vehicles which they use for the local journey to and from home. Others use minibuses for commuting. These car and minibus 'pools' are all privately organised. However, this creates a problem if they are travelling to suburbs like Arlington or Maclean in Virginia. Every car or minibus must have a minimum of three passengers or they are not allowed into the fast lane of the freeway in that state, a regulation scrupulously checked by the Highway Patrol. With the requisite three occupants, the vehicle may use the HOV lanes

The city of Washington, with its mass of flowering trees, provides an attractive setting for the crowds of children enjoying the Easter celebrations. On the lawns of the White House the Easter Bunny welcomes his guests who have come to find hidden chocolate eggs and play games with wooden ones. A distribution of cakes and sweets completes the day.

(High Occupancy Vehicle), which are designed to speed up the commute. Should a driver find himself below the three-person limit, he may pick up people who flag him down in the street – or even collect people from a bus stop.

Washington is a disconcerting city for many visitors because its centre is not a bustle of activity but an open green space 300 feet wide and a mile long. The Mall (pronounced 'maul') stretches from the Lincoln Memorial close to the Potomac, right up to the foot of Capitol Hill, the home of the American Congress. After passing the pale marble obelisk of the George Washington Monument, which has a lift inside to carry visitors the 555 feet to the top, the pedestrian runs the gauntlet of one of the most extraordinary concentrations of museum collections in the world.

The Smithsonian Institution is a monument to a legacy by a British scientist who never visited America and left a legacy 'to found in Washington, an establishment for the increase and diffusion of knowledge among men' on a whim. Once the ball had been set rolling, however, American benefactors and Congress soon got the idea and the network of museums and research institutes is now without parallel. Not only does the Smithsonian include the National Gallery of Art, the Freer collection of Oriental and Islamic art, the National Archive, the Air and Space Museum – which on its own gets more visitors (10 million a year) than any other museum in the world – it also owns the national zoo, the original Stars and Stripes and the world's largest stuffed elephant. Each month it publishes *Smithsonian* which, with a circulation of over 2 million, is America's leading cultural magazine. Without this great institution, Washington would be a very different city.

Visiting 'the Shore'

Although the capital is a busy city, it is also a small city and it is only a short drive from the centre to the open countryside. Going further afield, it is only two hours' drive to the beaches of Maryland and Virginia, always known as 'the Shore', which attract fishermen, naturalists, sailors and sunbathers.

In resorts such as Ocean City, Maryland, the beachside houses are small wooden huts with glazed porches. All built exactly alike, they can only be distinguished by the colours that they have been painted. One pale green number called 'The Birds' Nest' has been opened by a family who have come to stay the weekend. After dumping their bags indoors, everyone rushes off to the beach, the promenade or the quays. Separating the quiet beach from the bustle of the small town, the long boardwalk is the favourite meeting place for visitors. The aroma of tarred wood, salty air, pizzas and toasting popcorn mixes to create a characteristic smell. Small kiosks that sell the usual seaside paraphernalia line the boardwalk.

At regular intervals, jetties separate the beaches and sometimes run as much as a quarter of a mile out to sea for the benefit of the amateur fishermen. Solidly built from tarred logs, each jetty provides facilities for fishermen of all levels of experience. As soon as you step off the boardwalk, the intense silence is evident. Dozens of fishermen cast and recast their lines with total concentration. Among them, a small girl pulls a piece of string along very slowly, while another, beside her, hopefully clutches a landing-net. Suddenly, through the dark waters, the shadow of a large crab sidles up to the string. The landing-net slowly makes a circular movement and scoops him up while he is still nibbling the chicken neck tied to the end of the line.

There are so many crabs along this coast and they

The Appalachian Mountains are a stronghold of traditional folk music which is also popular in schools and colleges. This college choir travels from town to town singing their favourite numbers.

are so popular that some restaurants, called 'Crab Houses', serve nothing else. Once you have seated yourself, the waiter ties a large, thick cotton napkin round your neck and then sets a plateful of beautiful red crabs in front of you, together with salt and pepper, a knife, a small hammer and a tankard of cold beer to help lubricate the tubes. After dinner, a short stroll down the boardwalk will take you perhaps to an Irish bar where the songs break through the soft darkness. Meanwhile, the fishermen are still entrenched on the jetties, watching their lines or occasionally moving them in accordance with the ebb and flow of the tide. Some bars stay open all night, serving coffee and doughnuts to help the dedicated to stay awake until dawn.

The Blue Ridge Mountains of Virginia

While the sea draws those wanting a rest from the hot, humid summers of the cities, the Appalachian Mountains are a paradise for anyone able to extend their holidays to enjoy the splendours of the autumn colouring and the mild weather.

This is also the time of year for the tobacco sales. Some people say that Virginia was not only the earliest English colony in America and later the leader of the Southern states, but that it created the idea of monoculture by developing plantations whose economy was based on a single crop.

Tobacco was first tried in the coastal areas of

Maryland, but is now grown more successfully in southern Virginia, North Carolina and parts of South Carolina. However, it did not become a popular crop with farmers until the middle of the 19th century. Most tobacco is grown on relatively small farms, which can be distinguished by the presence of shiny new bulk-curing barns. Harvesting takes places over a period of four to eight weeks, during which time the pickers comb each field about once a week, looking for the ripe leaves at the base of the stalks. However, since 1970 the mechanisation of both picking and curing has increased so much that there has been serious depopulation in the tobacco-growing areas.

Outside Danville, in Virginia, a crowd is busy around an enormous shed: this is where the tobacco auction sales are held. Hundreds upon hundreds of piles of dried tobacco leaves are laid out, each packet marked with its weight, variety and the name of the farm where it was grown. The auctioneer makes his way down the lines, followed by a group of buyers. He pauses for barely a few seconds in front of each pile, calling out the successive numbers offered by the bidders, and in a few minutes 1000 lb of tobacco has been sold. One farmer's wife refuses the price offered, thinking it too low, and decides to wait for the next round of bidding. For the past 200 years, the famous golden Virginia tobacco has been sold in this way every autumn.

Up in the hills, the pale blue sky and bright air of the 'Indian summer' of Appalachia tempts the visitor into the territory of the ground squirrel and the garter snake. The flaming leaves of the oak and maple on the rolling slopes of the Blue Ridge Mountains flicker with every shade of yellow, orange and red. The best views can be had from the 105-mile-long Skyline Drive which runs along the top of the ridge. Driving along it, the visitor seems to look down from the 20th century into the untouched forests of prehistory.

Water power was the key to industrial progress before the development of the steam engine. Nowadays, families are finding that this endless source of cheap, non-polluting power helps to cut their electricity bills.

The dogwood grows wild in the southern states, but cultivated forms can be found in gardens and decorating the city streets. Its pink or white flowers are very attractive in the spring.

Fishing is a very popular pastime in the southern states. In the streams and rivers the quarry are trout, bass, walleye and channel catfish. The fish to go for in the lakes are largemouth bass, catfish and black crappie.

Sadly, this is a complete illusion as settlers long ago resorted to the slash-and-burn tactics that are currently raping the Amazon rain forest. What you see as you speed past in air-conditioned comfort is the result of the hard work and dedication of the National Forestry Service.

There is another side to this sylvan idyll, however. The forests overlay one of the world's richest sources of good-quality coal, and the Appalachians still yield about two-thirds of America's total output. Coal mining suffered a steady decline from the end of the Second World War until the early 1960s because its two biggest markets, the railways and domestic heating, were turning to alternative technologies. Then the demand for coal for electricity generating power stations began to grow, and the fading mining industry started to rally. The oil crisis of the early 1970s gave it an enormous shot in the arm, and coal production set new records. Unfortunately, this did not dent the

high levels of unemployment, particularly in West Virginia. About 60 per cent of the coal is extracted from strip mines which use colossal power shovels, the largest movable machines on Earth, which can extract 10,900 cubic yards an hour, to gouge out seams that are close to the surface. Where underground mining is necessary, the use of automated coal cutters make the man black with dust and a lamp on his head, as he hacks away at the coalface, a distant memory.

Beyond the western slopes of the Blue Ridge Mountains nothing seems to disturb the peace of the Shenandoah valley. Its inhabitants, unlike so many Americans who seem to be continually on the move, still live on the farms and lands colonised by their ancestors in the 18th century. In some isolated areas, the vocabulary and dialect of the locals seem to have more in common with 17th-century England than with 20th-century America.

The Shenandoah valley in Virginia rests under a slight mist which gives the Appalachian mountains their blue tinge. Hamlets, dotted about the valley among the apple orchards, add to the air of serenity.

The sound of success

Almost as old is the musical tradition that extends from West Virginia to the far ends of Tennessee. Nowadays country music's appeal is international, for wherever people need an instant identity and soothingly sentimental lyrics, from Tokyo to Tottenham, country music will find an audience. Perhaps that is appropriate, because the banjo was introduced by African slaves into Virginia, while the guitars and violins which dominate the country radio stations came from the Middle East via Europe.

Most of the performers hoping to make the big time in country music appear first in Nashville, Tennessee on the *Grand Ole Opry* – America's longest-running radio show. The programme is at the centre of a billion-dollar industry that has turned emotion into a commodity. There is even an Opryland theme park on the outskirts of the city. The Opry shows are given on Friday and Saturday nights but tickets are scarce.

Postmen have long distances to cover in rural areas so, to make things easier, letter-boxes are positioned at the roadside for the delivery man. If the owner has a letter to send, he puts up a small red flag on the side of the box. Each box is painted according to the owner's fancy with amusing abbreviations or designs.

Most houses in the South have their veranda. This is where the inhabitants welcome their friends, drink iced tea, and call from porch to porch as they exchange the latest news and welcome the little league baseball team that has come to ask for help in organising a picnic.

From West Virginia to Tennessee, music and songs are so popular that someone only has to start strumming on a banjo for a fiddler or a guitarist to join in.
These local groups are the foundation of the country-music industry that is based in Nashville.

The mineral-rich grass of Kentucky, on which the animals graze, helps this trainer to get the best out of his stable of horses which have been bred through a highly complex series of crosses to produce winners.

The stud farms of Kentucky provide better conditions for their horses than some people enjoy. This reflects the value of the fees that the owners can charge for the use of their stallions for breeding.

Disappointed fans can console themselves by a visit to the Country Music Hall of Fame, where they can see Chet Atkins's first guitar or Elvis Presley's gold-plated Cadillac. Most of the recording studios are located nearby on what has come to be known as Music Row – a square mile of talent, hype and hard work that runs south from Music Square Park. Amidst all the froth, the town still manages to record enough material to make it second only to Los Angeles in the American music business.

Authentic country music can still be found in the many tiny nightclubs scattered across Nashville. Real country music does not allow the use of electric guitars or percussion. It is played in the mountains, local people are its heroes, and its background is the hills of tall grass sprinkled with small blue flowers in the spring. This is why it is known as 'blue grass' music, the soul of the rolling mountains of Kentucky.

The Kentucky Stud

The famous Kentucky Derby Festival is held in Louisville on the first Saturday in May and attracts huge crowds every year. Before going to the races, a visit to the state's stud farms can be an eye-opener. The area round Lexington, about 80 miles east of Louisville, boasts at least 200 of these establishments, but only a few allow visitors.

Following the rolling hills leading to the farm,

the driveway is lined with seemingly endless white wooden fencing. Eventually you reach a model farm and discover what modern horse-raising is all about. The stables are air-conditioned and squeaky clean, the door handles are made of shining brass and the air is fragrant with fresh straw and clean leather. It all adds up to a luxury home for racehorses which have cost and will earn astronomical sums. In the adjoining meadows, the perfectly groomed horses nibble the famous 'blue grass' which is rich in the calcium and phosphates that will build them into champions. If one of these beauties pulls a muscle during a race, it will be sent off to be cured on a farm in Florida. There it will undergo a course of treatment, swimming daily in a special pool where the damaged leg can recover without further risk of strain. It is in places like this that champions such as Seattle Slew will end their days. Born in 1974, as a three-year-old he won the Derby, the Preakness and the Belmont Stakes and thus became one of the few horses ever to take America's Triple Crown. In 1978 his owners, who had paid 17,500 dollars for him, sold him for 12 million to a syndicate who will make that and much more from the stud fees.

The great day of the Louisville Derby is heralded by the warm spring sun. Churchill Downs, one of the most famous racecourses in America, is bright with flags, while the centre of the track is decorated with flowers. Behind the stands the crowd moves around inspecting the horses, admiring the favourites, appraising the unknowns or drinking a toast to the

The Kentucky Derby, the most famous race in the United States, is run in May. It is as much a social occasion as Royal Ascot, although it does not make such sartorial demands on the racegoers. After the race, winners and losers fill the restaurants of Louisville.

future winner. As in any American bar the choice is very liberal, but this is a good opportunity to sample a local favourite that its devotees claim is the only drink that really quenches your thirst: a mint julep. Correctly made of Kentucky bourbon whiskey, freshly picked mint and crushed ice, they say this cocktail can only be properly appreciated if you drink it in your own silver cup engraved with your initials.

At the crossroads of the South

Atlanta, Georgia is one the key symbols of the 'new South' and one of its great cities. Margaret Mitchell might have given it a big scene in *Gone with the Wind* but these days the citizens are more interested in business directories. With the offices of the trade delegations from over 30 different countries and the district offices of most of the world's great multi-nationals in town, Atlanta has little time to worry about the past, although a few of the colonial buildings which survived the Civil War still exist.

The city has one hometown multi-national all its own. In 1880 an enterprising inventor, Joseph Pemberton, created a new drink by combining an assortment of vegetable extracts, sugar, water and a little caramel in a saucepan at the back of his shop. This caramelised soda, flavoured with cola nut, acquired a trademark that has since become world-famous, while the recipe remains the secret of the Coca-Cola Corporation. The carbonated brown drink is the pride of Atlanta and in the vanguard of American trade throughout the world.

Atlanta did not exist before the railways came to Georgia and good transportation links still help the citizens to keep things moving. Hartsfield International Airport, located just south of the city, handled more than 11.5 million passengers in the first half of 1988, which makes it one of the busiest in the USA. During the same period, Kennedy Airport in New York dealt with about 7.5 million passengers. However, it is one thing to get people to Atlanta, and another to persuade them to stay. That is where air-conditioning, the technology that has transformed the South, has made the difference.

Atlanta has grown into a big modern city because it

In Atlanta, where 55 per cent of the population is black, these painted walls reflect the desire of these Americans for symbols of pride, now that they have achieved political power. Older citizens can remember the times when blacks were denied basic democratic rights and segregated on public transport.

The economy of the 'old South' was based on cotton and tobacco. With mechanisation, the harvesting of both crops can be done much faster, reducing the amount of labour required and increasing the profits. Farmers have diversified into cattle, turning the fields to pasture and ending years of soil erosion.

has been able to offer attractive working conditions to the executives who make the decisions in large companies. The Omni Complex, for example, has hotel facilities, offices, restaurants and shops in one completely enclosed, air-conditioned environment. It is connected to the Georgia World Congress Center next door, which is a major player in the massive business convention industry in the United States.

The Complex is just five blocks from the Peachtree Center, an air-conditioned shopping centre which occupies an entire city block. For the successful and affluent, Atlanta has created a protected environment which they hardly need to leave. With facilities like these on offer, the city is able to compete effectively for the new business of companies intending to set up shop in the South.

Florida: the rest-home with orange juice

The Greyhound bus stops at Orlando. Out gets a young man whose clothes and accent announce to everyone that he is Texan. Back home they laughed when he said he had decided to look for a job in Florida. 'They don't raise real animals there,' his friends declared with scorn, but they were wrong. The Deseret ranch, where he is going to work, fills most of the Kissimmee plain south of Orlando and belongs to the Mormons. The young man gets quite a surprise when he sees the herd but the foreman explains that they are a hybrid resulting from animals imported from India. A new breed called the Santa Gertrudis has been created that can stand up to the subtropical climate of Florida and still produce fine quality meat. It's all news to the young Texan but there will be plenty more he needs to get used to in the weeks ahead. He looks up just in time to see a flight of white pelicans passing overhead.

Florida is a creation of the 20th century. Most of the southern half of the peninsula was inaccessible swampland until Henry Flagler was persuaded to extend his railway south from Palm Beach to Miami. This allowed the orange growers of northern Florida, whose trees had been all but destroyed by frosts in the winter of 1894-5, to move to areas that were almost entirely frost-free. It also allowed hoteliers to move in and exploit the winter sunshine. Nowadays, the state has been transformed into a luxury resort where wealthy senior citizens retire and where those with a little less cash take a winter break.

As you leave Daytona and travel south, various billboards proclaim: 'You're getting nearer!', 'You're not far from the wonderful Walt Disney World', 'Visit Disney World'. Suddenly an enormous hamburger appears above the flat horizon. Maybe you are driving on automatic pilot and have begun day-dreaming. But as you draw nearer you realise that a small air-conditioned restaurant has been built inside the painted wooden hamburger. The effect is immediate: you stop and go in to eat a hamburger. Bombarded by publicity, holidaymakers are overwhelmed by the options open to them: would it be better to spend three days in Disney World, or would it be more fun to relax under the palm trees, two steps away from the latest Broadway successes in Miami Beach?

All these developments have placed a lot of pressure on the relatively small areas that were not swamp, but even the wetlands need protection. The Everglades National Park was created in 1947 to stop

This Florida motel advertises a heated pool so that its patrons can swim 'in all weathers' in a tropical climate!

Hollywood live! This water-ski spectacular is created for the holidaymakers who invade the resorts of Florida. What was scrubland has been transformed into a string of waterside playgrounds where the tourists outnumber the locals by up to 30 per cent every winter.

Florida's aquariums provide a rich variety of entertainment on and under the water. Through giant portholes in the sides of the tanks, visitors can observe the underwater life and watch divers feeding the fish. In a giant pool, a young killer whale is giving one of his keepers a ride.

Many of Florida's beachside apartment blocks have been built for the droves of the affluent who retire here to soak up the sun. In addition to the accommodation, swimming pools, tennis courts, golf courses and cinemas are provided.

estate agents nibbling away at the untouched swamp. However, it was not just a matter of stopping people building. More people needed more water and the new residents could not understand why some could not be taken from the Kissimmee River as there was so much water in Big Cypress Swamp in the west and the Everglades in the east. What they did not understand was that evaporation rates were so high that the swamps needed to be constantly topped up.

It was about this point that the Cuban revolution took place and immigrants arrived from the south as well as the north. The population just kept going up and up. In 1950, Florida was twentieth in a list of America's most populous states. By 1960 it was tenth. Twenty years later it was seventh. By 1990 it may well be fourth. In many areas around Miami, like many places in southern California, Spanish is the first language and some Americans cannot find work because they only speak English.

Despite this population influx there are still quiet, secluded places to be found. The shores of the Gulf of Mexico are quieter than the Atlantic coast. The water is pale blue, with pink flamingoes stalking over the white sand. If you take the ferry at Fort Myers which

crosses to the islands of Sanibel and Captiva, you may find the beach of your dreams – miles of sand showing nothing but your own footprints under the leaning palm trees.

If you are really lucky you might catch sight of a manatee, a large relative of the seal that has a paddle at the back instead of flippers. Its shape and its habit of resting half out of shallow water make it the most likely source of the legend of the mermaid. Other inhabitants of these warm coastal waters include dolphins, porpoises and turtles, while ospreys and eagles can be seen overhead.

Walkin' tall

'Texas is a state of mind' wrote John Steinbeck. Everything seems oversized and unreal, be it oil production, the cattle or the size of the hats which everybody seems to wear whether they are a garage owner, a shoe salesman or an engineer working in the space centre. Even the social occasions have a dream-like quality.

At Fredericksburg more than 30,000 Texans and a few 'foreigners' have gathered to celebrate the 'Sometimes Annual Luckenback World's Fair'. A mobile bottle of beer, twice the height of a man, comes over and points out where you can quench your thirst. Meanwhile, a loudspeaker is announcing the arrival of the musicians from Tennessee. Groups of dancers form up around the banjos and guitars. A little further away an animated discussion is being held on the subject of the preparation of the state's favourite dish: chili. This highly spiced, thick stew originated in Mexico but the question under discussion is whether onions are essential for a genuine chili and tempers are starting to get as hot as the food. Not far away a crowd has gathered around a mechanical 'bronco', a machine imitating the bucking and kicking of a wild horse. Loud whistles and enthusiastic shouts encourage anyone brave enough to try the mechanical beast.

Like the rest of the South, Texas has been transformed since the Second World War. Although oil and the petro-chemical industry are still at the heart of the state's economy, new arrivals have brought in people who do not resemble John Wayne or J. R. Ewing in the least. The establishment of the Space Center 25 miles south-east of Houston attracted the

Dallas, together with Houston, is the southern home of many great corporations. The headquarters of 18 of America's largest companies are located in these cities. Many other major businesses linked to oil, electronics and aerospace have built their regional offices here.

Industrialists in the South have turned to cattle-raising, almost as a hobby. They bring their taste for research and innovation with them and have helped to modernise farming practices in the area. Nowadays, cattle auctions are followed by receptions where a rancher in jeans would be out of place, although the traditional stetson is still much in evidence.

The bayou country of southern Louisiana is a swamp that is filled with grass and cypresses, patrolled by alligators and festooned with Spanish moss, which hangs down from the trees like green and grey streamers. It is also the land of the cajuns, those descendants of French settlers who have kept their unique dialect and their music and still hunt and fish in the land of their ancestors.

The Everglades National Park was created in 1947 in the south-west of Florida to protect the wildlife that relies on this wet wilderness for survival. Its 2188 square miles hold everything from the rare Florida panther to enormous shoals of fish. There are also 230 kinds of birds of all sizes – including the pelican and the pink flamingo, which are both strictly protected.

support services that any such facility needs to hand.

Contrary to popular myth, the American space programme has given more to the world than non-stick frying pans. The micro-miniaturisation of computers that was necessary to get men to the moon has changed the way the world works from airline sales counters to washing machines. Many of the American companies that make the microchips that

The big estates whose wealth came from cotton were like small towns with the master's house in the centre. Most of those that survive, like Oak Alley, have been turned into museums by their owners as a record of a past way of life.

The style of the girls' bedroom at Oak Alley Plantation gives an idea of what life was like for the owners of these vast domains. The doll wears a long dress and a lace bonnet, like those worn by the young girls of the period. They were carefully educated to enable them, in due course, to take their place as the mistress of a similar establishment.

French colonists named Louisiana after their king but it had a chequered history until it was sold to the United States by Napoleon in 1803. The Creole cuisine created by the descendants of its French and Spanish settlers has become world-famous.

drive these machines, like Motorola and Texas Instruments, have major plants around Houston and in the rest of the state.

Texan agriculture also fails to conform to its stereotypes. Cattle there are a-plenty, but the state is also a major producer of cotton. Until 1793, when Eli Whitney invented the cotton gin – a machine that separates the fibres from the cotton seed – cotton fabric was impossible to produce on an industrial basis. With that problem licked, the planters of Georgia and the Carolinas saw their opportunity, for most other crops had failed on their land. The plantation system which had been successful with tobacco was extended to the new crop and soon cotton was king throughout the South. But in 1892 disaster stuck when the boll weevil, a hungry little insect from Central America, first appeared and began to eat its way through the cotton fields and the profits. One way to hamper the pest was to move away from the habitats with high humidity that it prefers and irrigate the cotton bushes. This is why growers began moving to West Texas in the early years of this century. Nowadays, far more cotton is grown there than in the traditional areas such as Mississippi.

Posters on both sides of the street advertise jazz in the French quarter of New Orleans. These low houses with wrought-iron balconies have interior courtyards cooled by illuminated fountains and lit by torches. Here the best restaurants offer Creole cuisine and seafood specialities, followed by exotic desserts flavoured with rum and Caribbean fruit.

The successful fight for integrated education has enabled this little girl to benefit from a school serving the whole community, even if segregated private schools and universities still exist. Her printed skirt imitates patchwork which was originally designed to use up odd scraps of material. Bright colours and original design have made it a very fashionable pattern.

Dixieland jazz evolved as entertainment in the brothels of New Orleans, which were legal until 1917. Their closure at the insistence of the US Navy dispersed the musicians and spread their style throughout the country. Only when older musicians tired of travelling and returned to their homeland in the 1940s was the old style revived in the city of its birth.

Mardi Gras

Sitting on the terrace of a cafe near the old Place d'Armes in the French quarter of New Orleans, you can relax with a breakfast of coffee and croissants. The chill morning air is already heavy with the smells rising from the town and the river hidden behind the levees, the dykes that are used to control the waters of the great Mississippi.

Today is Shrove Tuesday, known here as Mardi Gras, and the quarter is still quiet. The narrow streets look very European with their old houses and their balconies of iron-lacework with pierced supports. Gradually, the city begins to stir. Today, even those who live in the ancient plantations of the surrounding country will leave their magnolia trees and moss-hung oaks to come to town.

The streets are slowly filling with carnival figures, and the procession of decorated cars will soon form.

Spectators crowd the pavements and lean from the upper windows, displaying the diversity and ethnic riches of Louisiana which belonged to the French, the Spanish and then the British before becoming American. The crowd on the streets are an animated reminder of this past, with faces in every shade from pale pink to dark brown – a spicy mixture of accents and inflections from the old world and the new.

The decorated cars arrive in a storm of shouting and clapping. The carnival kings scatter plastic golden coins struck in their likeness, and the crowd scrambles for this largesse as if it were real money. Meanwhile, down on Bourbon Street, halfway between the Mississippi and Louis Armstrong Park, there are plenty of young women who are profiting from the large crowds to indulge in a little private enterprise. Until 1917, prostitution was quite legal in the French quarter and it is still conducted today. New Orleans likes to support the oldest traditions.

The Preservation Hall Jazz Band of New Orleans is undoubtedly one of the longest established in existence. It operates in a small room in the French quarter, with decorations unchanged for decades.

The Home of Liberty

On July 4, 1776, in Philadelphia, the thirteen American colonies rebelling against British rule declared their independence. Here, on the north-east coast of the continent, a nation was born that was the first to affirm that men have the right not only to life and liberty but also – an unprecedented assumption – to pursue happiness. The ringing phrases which were used in that declaration have been an inspiration to people around the world ever since.

> *We hold these truths to be self-evident: that all men are created equal, that they are endowed by their Creator with certain inalienable rights: among these are Life, Liberty and the pursuit of Happiness. That to secure these rights, Governments are instituted among Men, deriving their just powers from the consent of the governed. That whenever any Form of Government becomes destructive of these ends, it is the Right of the People to alter or abolish it, and to institute new Government, laying its foundation on such principles and organizing its powers in such form, as to them shall seem most likely to effect their safety and Happiness.*

The colonies of the north-east were key participants in the North American experiment from the moment that the pilgrims of the *Mayflower* landed at Plymouth, about 35 miles south of what is now Boston in December 1620. After leaving England a few months earlier in search of religious freedom, the 102 settlers arrived on this wild coast bordered by forests filled with native people of unknown intentions. The local Indian people had been decimated by illness in the years before the landing, however, and they offered no immediate threat. Virginia had been the settlers' intended destination, but storms and poor navigation cast them on a different shore. They accepted their fate and settled down to worship God and plant their crops. Their ascetic puritanism raised no objections to hard work and the pursuit of profit. The seeds of the future were starting to take root.

Their new home posed few serious threats to the settlers. The landscape was not unduly hostile and the climate was not so different from the one which the settlers had left. Ten years later, Boston was founded; even today the surrounding countryside is still a green and pleasant land with rolling hills, forests and pastures dotted with small white houses.

New Yorkers would be lost without Central Park. This green space in the centre of Manhattan provides lawns and shady groves where they can relax, as well as ponds, sports fields, an ice rink, a museum and even a zoo.

But it is the extent of its urban development that distinguishes the north-eastern United States at the end of the 20th century. Cities and suburbs stretch out towards one another along a coastal corridor that extends from Boston in the north to Washington in the south. Geographers increasingly call the region 'Megalopolis', although it still has enough greenery to make a little space between the strips of asphalt and the fingers of concrete.

A hard land for tough people

Huge rust-coloured round rocks lie piled at the foot of headlands, washed by the Atlantic spray. Long creeks with water of a dazzling blue reflect the pines that cover hundreds of islands or a whole archipelago like Mount Desert Island, where the Acadia National Park can be found. However, if Maine's coastline looks like that of Sweden, its interior looks more like Finland, with many lakes and immense forests of pine – white, red and grey – flourishing alongside hawthorn, balsam, poplars and birch trees. The forests have earned Maine the title of the Pine Tree State.

It is certainly very beautiful country but that does not stop the locals complaining about the winters. 'Nine months of winter and three months when you can't put a sleigh outdoors', runs a local saying. In fact, the winters last from October to March or April. Everything is covered in snow but most people are prepared, even though pipes freeze from time to time and the weather varies a lot. One day a blizzard strikes and blots out mountains and valleys. Next morning, perhaps the sun will rise in a sky of Mediterranean blue, revealing a dazzling landscape. However, the most beautiful time of year is the autumn. In the tangled forests the maples blaze with reds, oranges and yellows above the golden bracken while the air is extraordinarily mild.

Maine, which was christened by pioneers coming from the French province of the same name who attempted to settle there in 1604, starts about 50 miles north of Boston and extends to the Canadian border. Indeed, its people frequently seem to have more in common with their friends in the Canadian Maritimes than with many of the citizens of the other 49 states. For example, they are more interested in fishing than in factory work and their coastal waters are alive with lobsters, just like those north of the border. This is a big attraction to the swarms of tourists that visit the area every year.

New Hampshire, the other holiday state, is much more rugged. It has even been called the 'American Switzerland', although such a title is somewhat fanciful: its highest peak, Mount Washington is only 6289 feet high. Its bare summit, usually shrouded in mist

New Hampshire has more than 1300 lakes and countless waterways. For the many tourists who visit the state, skiing is popular in winter, while fishing, swimming and other watersports are favoured in summer. Alternatively, they can explore its white houses, old covered bridges and immaculate farms.

Pumpkin pie is one of the most traditional American dishes and a favourite on Thanksgiving Day, one of America's great national holidays, held on the fourth Thursday in November.

New England still has plain, elegant houses built of painted wood with carved pediments. The first pioneers lived in log cabins and, in a land rich in timber, wood continues to be the cheapest construction material.

Americans are surrounded by so much space, even in the crowded north-east corridor, that only determined city dwellers need live in apartments. Suburbs spread out round all major cities because so many people want a detached house, however small, on its own plot of land.

or lashed by the wind, and for that reason known locally as 'Misery Mountain', looks like a piece of Labrador that has drifted off to the south. It forms part of the White Mountains in the north-east of the state and notices in the area warn tourists: 'Attention: you are entering the most dangerous climatic zone in the United States! Many hikers have died of cold, even in summer. Go back if the weather is bad!'

The rain in Maine

Two forest rangers are almost hidden by the deep afternoon shadow as they follow the access trail between the stands of pine and white birch. Walking with their heads to one side, they are trying to gauge how serious the problem really is. The ragged tips of the treetops are a giveaway that all is not well. What with the cold and the thin soil, even the pines have a tough time here. But that is not what concerns them now; this area was where the phenomenon of acid rain first became apparent.

Much of the atmospheric pollution appears to blow in from the industrial zones of the Mid-West. The sulphur dioxide from power plants and factory chimneys is dissolved in the atmospheric moisture, together with the nitrous oxide fumes emitted by these industrial sources and by cars. This makes the moisture held in clouds more acidic than normal and when rain falls the landscape suffers. Many soils are unaffected by this problem because they are naturally alkaline and neutralise the rainwater, but this does not happen in New England. Many of the lakes in the region are so acidic that they can barely support any form of life. Local people became so sensitive to the issue that more than half the towns in

This old fisherman mending his net is the symbol of a declining industry. For 300 years fishing was the main occupation for most New Englanders, and the fleets brought back tons of cod from the Newfoundland Banks. But Canada has extended its territorial limits, and Americans no longer have access to these rich fishing grounds.

New Hampshire had their own acid rain monitoring systems, while most of the television stations in Maine broadcast measurements of the acidity of the rain regularly rather like the pollen count in Britain. Although there are no mysteries about solving the problem, the installation of pollution control systems would be very costly and so the idea has not been very popular with politicians. Their survey done, the two rangers get into their large estate waggon and drive back to base. As they disappear in the distance, a pale blue haze of exhaust fumes drifts away from the road and is dispersed by the breeze.

In 1620 the Mayflower pilgrims landed on Cape Cod in south-east Massachusetts, not far from where this fisherman's house stands. The peninsula has become a favourite resort for painters as well as for rich Bostonians, who come here for sailing holidays and have built themselves magnificent villas.

Lobsters are a Maine speciality, although they are less plentiful than they used to be along the coast. They have become a bit more expensive, but they are still reasonably priced. They are always available in the local seafood restaurants, which offer fish and shellfish of all kinds.

The witches' brew

Massachusetts is the heart of New England and its historic basis. Apart from Boston, there are numerous smaller towns and villages grouped round their churches, with colonial-style houses and beautifully kept lawns. Once the grass has been cut every Sunday, the chairs and tables are set out and if the weather is fine, everybody eats outdoors. In this patrician state, traditions are cultivated the way other people grow potatoes.

Glossy Massachusetts with its electronics factories and bio-technology corporations may seem the last place anyone would go in search of superstition nowadays, but matters were somewhat different in the 17th century. Between May and October 1692, 19 inhabitants of Salem, a town about 12 miles north of Boston, were hanged as convicted witches, while many others were persecuted for their alleged involvement. The situation arose after a West Indian slave, Tituba, incited some girls to accompany her into the forest and undress in order to participate in some rituals akin to the voodoo ceremonies of her homeland. When these events came to public notice in the repressive Puritan atmosphere of 17th century New England, the girls could only deflect the wrath of their elders by claiming that they had been possessed by the Devil. In this inflamed atmosphere accusations soon began flying, frequently being used to settle old scores between some of the women involved. Magistrates, encouraged by the clergy, set up a special court and soon events got completely out of hand. The witch hunts were only halted when public opinion turned against the judges. Such mass hysteria was also common in Scotland but Salem is probably remembered because it provided Arthur

Miller, one of America's greatest 20th-century playwrights, with the outline for one of his most successful plays, *The Crucible*, which he used to attack the anticommunism hysteria of the early 1950s.

The ignorance and isolation of such communities is difficult to believe now but before 1775 the economy of Massachusetts was entirely rural, being based on cattle and fishing. When London's control of its colonies was broken by the War of Independence, however, the Americans were free to develop as they wished; Boston's merchants took their chance to invest in textile and leather factories, both of which could obtain their raw materials locally. However, as the 19th century wore on, industry in general increasingly turned to coal and iron, raw materials which were not found in New England. Industrial areas in the south and west outstripped those places that had developed first. By the beginning of the 20th century, New England was not merely stagnating, it was actually losing business, a process that accelerated as time passed. By the end of the Second World War the situation was desperate. Boston had to act before it became completely deindustrialised.

One of the state's prime assets has always been its educational community. The town of Cambridge houses the Massachusetts Institute of Technology and Harvard University, founded in 1636 and endowed by a British clergyman, John Harvard, who left his library and half his fortune to the first major college in North America. These two world-famous institutions became the focus of efforts to develop commercial openings based on the latest technologies, mainly electronics. The success of this initiative was so great that Boston and its ring road, Route 128, where most of the new factories have been located, have become synonymous with those developing sectors that are known as 'sunrise' industries and are held up as an example, both in Europe and America, to those areas in decline as a way to revive their flagging fortunes.

Boston's Old State House, built in the Dutch style in 1713, was the Governor's residence before the 13 colonies seceded. The Declaration of Independence was read from its balcony in 1776. Now a museum, it is flanked by tall buildings proclaiming Boston's success as a commercial and industrial centre.

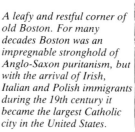

A leafy and restful corner of old Boston. For many decades Boston was an impregnable stronghold of Anglo-Saxon puritanism, but with the arrival of Irish, Italian and Polish immigrants during the 19th century it became the largest Catholic city in the United States.

The business of learning

Harvard is one of the richest universities in the United States with assets recently valued at more than 4200 million dollars. All the private American universities charge substantial tuition fees. Harvard, for example, costs each student over 19,300 dollars a year, while the most expensive, Bennington College in Vermont, charges over 19,975 dollars. Universities also benefit from legacies from former students or gifts provided by individuals or corporations.

Nowadays, Boston is enjoying its revived prosperity. The Faneuil Hall Marketplace, built in 1826 not far from City Hall, was completely refurbished between 1976 and 1978, attracting a new generation of shoppers. Even the city's basketball team, the Celtics, has been resuscitated and has appeared in many world championships in recent years. However, some things never seem to change.

Beacon Hill, overlooking the Charles River Basin, has been been the home of the city's leading families, the so-called Boston Brahmins, for generations. This is the closest the United States comes to an aristocracy and the cobbled streets with their elegant townhouses, graced by immaculate brass knockers make this crystal clear.

While these families were becoming established on the hill in the 18th century, a man with very different allegiances was living in a wooden house in North End down by the river. Paul Revere was a member of republican groups and a trusted courier for many years before the War of Independence. His most famous ride was provoked by the Governor of Massachusetts, General Gage, who despatched British troops to seize a cache of arms held by disaffected Americans on the evening of April 18, 1775. Revere's midnight dash to rouse the sleeping farmers of Lexington succeeded and the following morning a ragged skirmish between the two groups signalled the beginning of the War of Independence.

The chimes of freedom ringing

Contrary to legend, the famous Liberty Bell was not rung on July 4, 1776 to summon the citizens of Philadelphia to hear the first reading of the Declaraion of Independence – for the simple reason that the signatures necessary for the ratification of the document were not collected that day. Only on July 8 was the bell heard when the declaration was read from a temporary platform erected outside the State House. Nevertheless, the bell is piously preserved in a glass pavilion across the road from Independence Hall, a small building topped by a modest bell-tower where that second great document, the Constitution of the United States, was drawn up in 1787. Independence Hall stands beside Congress Hall, the seat of the Federal Government from 1790 to 1800, and the old Town Hall which housed the Supreme Court, until the country's ultimate source of legal authority moved to Washington. The whole of Pennsylvania seems awash with history in a way that is unusual in the United States. Pittsburgh still carries the name of the 18th-century British prime minister who was in charge when the French were ousted from the area in 1758. The town's position astride the junction of the Monongahela and Allegheny Rivers, the keys to transportation in the interior at the time, ensured that it expanded by leaps and bounds after enormous coal reserves were found nearby just two years later. The later discovery of iron ore in the area turned Pittsburgh into America's industrial heartland. By

This narrow, cobbled street on Beacon Hill is the home of some of the most exclusive families in the United States. Its terraced houses ascend one of the three hills on which Boston is built, and many are owned by those who pride themselves on being descended from the religious refugees who founded the New England colony in the 17th century.

the 1920s, the city's furnaces were making as much steel as France, Japan, Sweden and Germany combined. For decades, the industry was dominated by one company, US Steel, which manipulated politicians and the forces of law and order in Pennsylvania to its own advantage. Only in 1962, after it had been humiliated in public by President Kennedy in a confrontation over steel prices, was the company's power finally broken. Nowadays, as in steel towns throughout the world, many of Pittsburgh's blast furnaces have been closed as overcapacity in the early 1980s caused cutbacks everywhere, particularly among old plants.

In 20 years time they will be executives or lawyers with cars to wash and lawns to mow, following a career that was based on graduating from one of America's great universities.

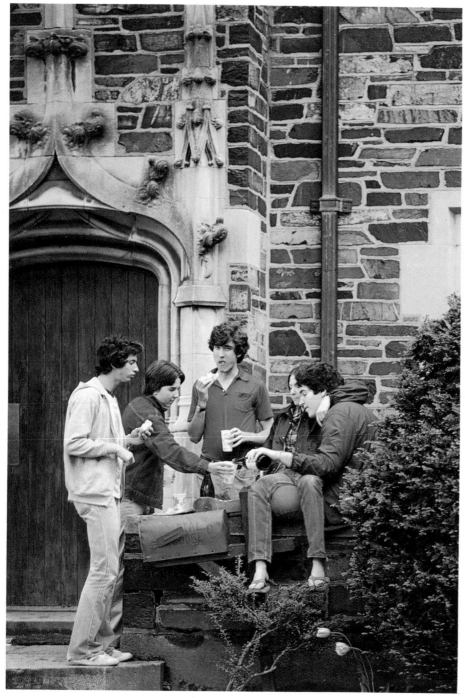

The plain people

In the rolling farmland not too far from the Susquehanna River, the sun is rising and has just touched the biscuit-coloured wooden barns grouped on the edge of a coppice. The only sounds are those of a bird singing on the wing and the clip clop of a horse trotting down the lane. The small carriage rolling along behind it holds a couple and their three children. As they disappear into the distance, the broad back of the head of the family, clad in the black suit he wears every day, is visible in the front seat, next to his young son, also in a black suit and black, broad-brimmed hat. Behind him sits his wife and their two daughters, clad in white bonnets. They are off to the meeting house for the weekly service with its sermon delivered in an odd mixture of English and German. These are the Pennsylvania Dutch. Intent on escaping the religious persecution they had endured in their homelands, they arrived from Germany and Switzerland in the 18th century. They were drawn to the area because William Penn, who had obtained a charter from Britain's Charles II in 1681, had based his colony on religious tolerance, being a Quaker himself. The first settlements thrived because they had been fortunate enough to find agricultural land of the highest quality. When the new settlers arrived, their already established colleagues were unable to say 'Deutsch' clearly and so the Germans became Dutch.

Outside the meeting house, the sermon over, the men have drifted into groups and are discussing the crops. Although this community rejects the paraphernalia of the 20th century – its cars and tractors, telephones and televisions – it does not mind exploiting the enormous market for tobacco that has developed in the last 100 years and that is its main cash crop. When the men are seen together, it is soon apparent that the full beard but shaved upper lip is the prerogative of every married man and has a particular significance. These are the Amish, a breakaway group that found too many of the original

settlers were backsliding and accepting too many compromises to their Bible-based, Mennonite faith, which was once described as 'God said it. Jesus did it. I believe it. And that settles it.' Like the Quakers, they are pacifists and regard moustaches as having military connotations. However, their less strict neighbours in southern Pennsylvania are not averse to a little 20th-century-style capitalism and the town of Hershey is the home of the famous chocolate bar, the essential prop in any Second World War movie.

Philadelphia today – William Penn's 'city of brotherly love' – is also a community with strong roots in the past that has a viable commercial heart. It has its beautifully preserved 18th-century housing on Society Hill overlooking the Delaware River. Around Independence Square, Elfreth's Alley, one of the oldest streets in the United States, recalls the charms of colonial life with its 30-odd brick houses dating from 1762 with the gutter running down the middle of the street. But the city is also a great manufacturing centre and an important port due to its position on the Delaware River, even though it is nearly 100 miles from the sea. Sadly, it also has its ghettos for the poor and underprivileged.

Outside, the mellow spring evening makes driving home a joy. On either side, the mature gardens of this leafy suburb of 'Philly' conceal a touch of England in the architecture. Here and there one admires the discreet use of 'Tudor' beams on the exterior. The pink and white blossom of the magnolia and cherry trees set off the dark oak panelling of the large double garages. The problem in Merion is finding opponents whom they can challenge to a game of cricket.

This attachment to England is a strong undercurrent among the wealthy of America's East Coast. Down in Delaware, the Du Ponts, the creators of the giant chemical company, have expended vast sums on transplanting an English-style garden to the New World. Even New York City's Central Park has a group of enthusiasts who replanted a garden with herbaceous borders in the early 1980s. Unfortunately, such endeavours will never be entirely successful because the sudden warmth of the East Coast spring brings on plants with such a rush that roses come out with azaleas and by July, flowers that would be approaching their moment of glory in England, need to be dead-headed in New Jersey.

A corner of a foreign land

Nobody is in a state of need at the Merion Cricket Club – unless, that is, they want a little more salad with their steak. Their clubhouse has played host to the smiling faces of many famous sportsmen and now the photographs that recorded those visits grace its walls. Before the tennis circuit became such big business, the club hosted one of the major annual tournaments. It was here that one of the greats of golf, Bobby Jones, won his last US Amateur Open in the early 1930s on one of their two courses. It is the maintenance of such traditions and the upholding of certain standards which make the club a pillar of the Merion set.

Harvard University just across the Charles River from Boston in the town of Cambridge, is the oldest of the American universities. Founded in 1636, it numbers the poet Longfellow and President Kennedy among its alumni. Its campus is attractive and well-established, with one building going back to 1720.

The style of graduation day is emphatically Anglo-Saxon for these American students who walk in procession wearing cap and gown. Parents heave sighs of relief on this day, for they have often had to make substantial financial sacrifices to put their child through such a prestigious establishment.

Sightseers ascend a spiral staircase inside the Statue of Liberty to reach the observation platform inside its crown. This symbol of democratic freedom, which has attained a universal significance, has stood upon its pedestal overlooking New York Harbour since 1886.

Long legs and a piece of taffy

As the Greyhound bus approaches Atlantic City, it is possible to wonder whether the driver has taken the wrong road; the surrounding landscape looks so featureless and empty. Even the bus station is rather small and down-at-heel. But it is only as you approach the ocean that you can see the new buildings that have helped to change the city's image since 1976.

For decades until the Second World War, Atlantic City reigned supreme as America's most famous playground. Its proximity to the big cities of the East Coast gave it a ready clientele before the age of jet airliners. However, once Americans were able to

The terrace on the roof of a New York apartment block overlooking Columbus Circle, complete with artificial grass, provides the residents with an opportunity to sunbathe without leaving the city. Their modest swimwear is typically American.

move around their nation with greater ease, Atlantic City's star began to wane. The previously elegant hotels were fading fast when the voters of New Jersey agreed to create a special dispensation for the town in a referendum held in 1976. Nowhere else outside Nevada is casino gambling legal in the USA.

Within 18 months the first purpose-built casino had opened its doors, and by 1984 the city's annual gambling revenues had surpassed those of Las Vegas. Although organised crime has undoubtedly funded some of the building programme, New Jersey has kept its hand on the tiller and insists that its original intentions are observed. These involve the construction of a minimum of 500 first-class hotel rooms in every new casino. New Jersey fully intends to establish Atlantic City on the business convention circuit, the lucrative trade that has done Atlanta so much good.

Meanwhile, much of the business is based on day-trippers because so many people live within an easy drive of the resort. The doors of all the casinos face onto the boardwalk, the six-mile-long wooden walkway that stands on stilts, gazing down on the beach. In times past, it was *the* place to promenade with your folks. Nowadays, its where you go to cool off after the excitement of the tables.

The main door of the casino is normally on the other side of the building, facing the street or the car

park. Once inside, it is just a short escalator ride up to the main gambling floor. At the top, you pass a number of large men whose function is not entirely clear. Are they really underworld 'heavies' or are they part of the furnishings, in position to look sinister and persuade you that you are about to do something really naughty? Through another set of doors, acres of one-armed bandits seem to go on forever, for the walls are lined with mirrors.

Beyond the machines are the roulette and blackjack tables. However, it is the craps pits that get the customers on their toes. Here the customers roll dice, trying to get certain combinations, while everyone around the game bets on the outcome. This is a friendly game because the gamblers are always urging on the roller, muttering their own favourite incantations that they just know are going to change the outcome.

To get a drink you try to catch the attention of the waitresses, who circulate in high-heeled shoes, dark tights and costumes with pieces of fur attached in provocative positions. Although the drinks are free, it is considered proper etiquette to drop one of your chips on her tray as a tip. To get something to eat here, you have to visit the balcony that overlooks the players. To get to it you use another short

The beautiful Brooklyn Bridge, which spans the East River, still carries plenty of commuter traffic to and from Manhattan despite its age. Construction of this suspension bridge, which is over 1¼ miles long, was completed in 1883. A walkway gives pedestrians a splendid view of Manhattan and New York Harbour.

Like all big cities, New York has serious traffic problems. As parking is very difficult in Manhattan, relatively few people who live there own their own car, preferring to hire one should they need to travel out of town.

escalator. On either side of this moving stairway is a waterfall, tumbling down as you ascend. This really is fantasyland.

On the boardwalk, the Atlantic breezes blow all the cobwebs away. Here, the entertainments that were at their prime decades ago still linger in places. The shops and kiosks still sell what is known as saltwater taffy, which is a sort of fudge. These days the packaging reflects the new money in town – glossy white card with black dots folded into a very large dice shape.

Peter Minuit's bargain

A large percentage of the people leaving Atlantic City head north. They are being drawn back to one of the most magnetic places on Earth. New York City originally meant the island of Manhattan. Today, four other boroughs – the Bronx, Queens, Brooklyn and Richmond – have been added, sharing a city council, but each with its own individuality, loyalties, traditions and accents.

Settlement began when a Dutchman called Peter Minuit bought Manhattan from the Algonquin Indians in 1626 for the equivalent of 26 dollars worth

The New York cop, popularised in so many movies, was traditionally Irish. Nowadays recruiting is more diversified, with increasing numbers of black or Puerto Rican policemen on the streets.

of glass beads and hardware. Some people have seen this as a confidence trick: the sophisticated operator cheating the trusting native out of his birthright. In fact it was nothing of the sort for the Dutch very soon realised that the chief who had sold them the island was not the real owner and they had to fight off the claims of another Indian tribe in order to keep it. The sophisticated European had been duped. Less than 40 years later, the English seized the colony of New Netherland and changed the name of its capital, New Amsterdam, to New York in honour of Charles II's brother, the Duke of York.

But New York is not just a city. The city is part of a state which is half the size of the United Kingdom. Indeed, the contrast between the city and its rural hinterland could not be much greater. The state is for those love the open air and is much enjoyed by hikers in summer as well as skiing enthusiasts in winter, for it is quite mountainous.

Taking the train from Grand Central Station is the most relaxed way to get out of town. Just an hour's travel takes you on the elevated tracks across Harlem, off the island and into the foothills of the Catskill Mountains.

The towns of Connecticut, such as New Haven and Meriden, also feature heavily on the destination boards at Grand Central Station. This state, which borders Long Island Sound and extends up to Massachusetts from a point about 20 miles north-east of Manhattan, acts as a dormitory and a playground for New Yorkers.

Hartford, the state capital, is the headquarters of many insurance companies. It was also the home of Samuel Colt, who was one of the first to bring standardised production techniques into engineering in his small arms factory. The development of such manufacturing methods brought his handgun, the Colt revolver, into the price range of those who previously could not have considered the purchase of a hand-crafted weapon. In so doing, he changed the history of the settlement of the American West and the mythology that surrounds it. The State Library Museum in Hartford has a permanent exhibition of Colt revolvers.

November 11 is known as Veterans' Day and is used to honour ex-servicemen. Associations that look after their interests are very powerful. The first was formed for veterans of the War of Independence, while the most famous, the American Legion, was created after the First World War. Now the veterans of the Second World War have been joined in its ranks by their comrades from the wars in Korea and Vietnam.

New Yorkers are used to dealing with idiosyncratic people. Nobody is in the least surprised to see a priest preaching on the street. Spectators listen politely, with amusement or indifference.

Despite the promise of the American Dream, many fail to benefit from it.

The big apple

New York is not concerned primarily with history. It has kept only a few traces of its past which might disappear from one day to the next – like Trinity Church, an Anglican church on Wall Street, the heart of the financial district and home of the New York Stock Exchange. Wall Street is a curious little dog-leg that twists between massive piles of stone and concrete. As one of the homes of world banking it is sometimes rather limited, as anyone who tries to cash anything other than dollar travellers cheques will find out.

Getting around New York City takes a little skill and can be intimidating for the beginner. The subway is very badly signposted, very noisy and very frightening, especially if you have seen it in the movies. However, the chance of your train being hijacked, seeing policemen running around waving guns or people jumping on and off trains in order to shake off pursuers is very remote. The reality is much more mundane, but it can be just as scary.

New Yorkers demonstrate for such unexpected causes that it is frequently very difficult to know whether they are serious or playing a joke.

A quiet Sunday afternoon

If New York was all fear and confrontation, people would have moved away long ago. Yet, despite periodic municipal bankruptcy, garbage collection strikes, poor roads, drugs and organised crime, the city is still number one, both economically and intellectually, in the United States. If you are in the clothing business, shipping, publishing, finance, the theatre or fine art, New York is the place to be, the city where reputations are made and lost.

New York acts like a magnet to the talented and the ambitious, and with so many people eager to get ahead, things happen faster than elsewhere. One telephone call can set up in a matter of hours a business deal or an interview that might take days in other cities. All this creates a very energetic atmosphere that is highly conducive to work. Thus, although the city has such outstanding museums as the Metropolitan and the Whitney, the Statue of

The town of Nieuw Haarlem was founded in 1658 by the Dutch. But as New York expanded during the 19th century, the renamed Harlem became a fashionable residential suburb of Manhattan. When the residents of the neighbourhood moved out to the newer suburbs beyond the East River, they were replaced by affluent blacks who, in the 1920s, turned Harlem into the first great centre of black culture. Only later, when absentee landlords packed in as many tenants as they could while spending as little as possible on the buildings, did the district degenerate into a slum.

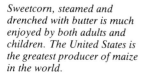

Sweetcorn, steamed and drenched with butter is much enjoyed by both adults and children. The United States is the greatest producer of maize in the world.

Baseball can seem a little confusing to the uninitiated, but games are watched with passionate interest all over North America, especially when the winners of the two major leagues meet in the World Series.

The black churches have been a great force for good in American society during the 20th century, giving cohesion and strength to a community under stress and in transition. It is no coincidence that the greatest black leader, Martin Luther King, rose to lead the civil rights movement from his position as a preacher.

Vietnam veterans, the neglected heroes of a generation, receive a rapturous ticker-tape reception from New Yorkers.

Liberty and the theatres of Broadway, it has never been a tourist town in the same way as Washington, London or Paris. New York is a place where people come to live and work.

It is four o'clock on a Sunday afternoon and an English couple are crossing a windy Sixth Avenue. The man is clutching a piece of paper on which an address has been scribbled and is looking round in disbelief. Surely this cannot be the place? They are in the middle of the garment district and the street is deserted. However, just as they were told, between two seedy shop fronts a door is ajar. They go up two flights and enter a different world. This is a New York loft.

The enormous room, which now has a pale, polished wood floor, was once one of the local sweat shops. Where industrial sewing machines stood, there is a kitchen area where some of the guests are selecting their food from a variety of wooden bowls. At the other end of the bare room are a large bed and some armchairs. Everyone seems very relaxed as the host, Marvin, who runs one of Manhattan's best uptown art galleries, greets the couple. The Englishman is soon talking to the art director of one of the top American photographic magazines. Within half an hour he appears to have been offered a regular monthly column on events in London. His partner, meanwhile, is chatting to a South African woman who works at the Metropolitan Museum of Art. Perhaps she would like to come uptown tomorrow and take a look at their prints. Doing business in New York can sometimes be a very civilised affair.

The hope of liberty

The United States of America is a land of immigrants and New York is the port through which many of them first entered the country. In the middle of the 19th century, the Irish poured through its docks to escape from the famine that scourged their land. At the end of the century it was the turn of southern and eastern Europe to flee to the land of opportunity. Their numbers were so great that a special reception centre was opened on Ellis Island in the harbour opposite Manhattan to process them as they arrived.

Those days are long since gone, but immigrants are still arriving. Despite the imposition of legal controls, the human tide receded only in the 1930s when the United States was in the grip of a recession. During the 1980s, the numbers of immigrants has swollen again to the point where an average of half a million people are gaining permanent residence every year. These days the immigrants come from a variety of countries, with Vietnam, the Dominican Republic, India and Mexico contributing large numbers. The Spanish-speaking settlers have tended to congregate in specific areas and there are large concentrations in Florida, Texas, California and New York City, where they have their own television channels, politicians and businesses using their native language.

The aim of these immigrants is to secure their family's future. Any of their children born in the United States automatically become citizens, but the first generation immigrants have to petition for naturalization. If they are married to an American

The Easter Day Parade on New York's Fifth Avenue is the scene of a traditional display which goes back to the days when the richest families lived in Manhattan. The normally busy street is closed all morning so that everyone can promenade in clothes that vary from the stylish to the bizarre.

A gala at the Metropolitan Museum brings together New York's rich and famous. All American museums are heavily dependent on the donations of rich citizens to keep afloat. Such support is encouraged by the Federal Government which makes such contributions tax deductible.

citizen they can make their application after three years, otherwise they have to remain in the country for five years.

Annita da Paulo has lived in the United States for nine years, working as the assistant to a businessman who owns a number of student hostels in Nevada and Washington, DC. He has just bought a small hotel in Manhattan and Annita is going to manage it. She comes from Brazil where she and her brother ran a business in the south of the country. After the security of her life in America, she does not wish to return to the financial chaos of her native land.

The first stage of the naturalization process involves filing an application which means that two forms have to be filled out and a fingerprint card completed. These are sent to the Immigration and Naturalization Service who then notify the applicant when they must come before a naturalization examiner. The examiner will ask a number of simple questions about the history of the United States to demonstrate the applicant's interest in their new country and their command of English. The examiner also ensures that any titles of nobility or marks of status held by them in their former country are renounced. The applicant is then helped to fill out the legal document known as the petition of naturalization and a small fee is paid.

All the preliminary stages are done and all the form-filling is over. This is Annita's day in the Federal Court in Brooklyn. She and her teenage daughter Tania, who is spending a year in New York to learn English, arrive early and sit in the back of the room. With so many immigrants living in the New York area, applicants are dealt with in groups. The room is quite full before the judge finally enters. Annita smiles nervously at her daughter and steps forward. The naturalization examiner is present and affirms to the court that all those named have been found qualified for naturalization and should be made citizens. The Clerk of the Court then reads out the oath, which Annita and the other applicants repeat after him.

I hereby declare, on oath, that I absolutely and entirely renounce and abjure all allegiance and fidelity to any foreign prince, potentate, state or sovereignty, of whom or which I have heretofore been a subject or citizen; that I will support and defend the Constitution and laws of the United States of America against all enemies, foreign and domestic; that I will bear true faith and allegiance to the same; that I will bear arms on behalf of the United States when required by the law; that I will perform noncombatant service in the armed forces of the United States when required by the law; that I will perform work of national importance under civilian direction when required by the law; and that I take this obligation freely without any mental reservation or purpose of evasion; so help me God.

The judge nods. 'Thank you ladies and gentlemen, you are now citizens of the United States.' Annita returns to her daughter smiling but biting her lip. Now, anything is possible.

During the 19th century, many wealthy American women adopted a role that emphasised the joining of social clubs and associations devoted to particular causes. The pattern spread down the generations and today many women, instead of relaxing in their retirement, indulge in an endless whirl of activity.

Canada

Advancing from pioneer cabins to microchip sophistication
in just a few generations, Canadians are building one nation
out of a multitude of languages and many traditions.
Amid 3.5 million square miles of wheatfields, forests and lakes,
a future is being created in which individual freedom
and minority cultures are treated with the same respect
as the nation's economic health.

In the tundra close to the Arctic Circle, the ground is frozen most of the year and nothing grows except mosses and lichens. The population is very scattered, consisting mainly of Indians.

The elegant gannet travels the North Atlantic coastline searching for fish which it spears by diving from a height, closing its wings as it hits the water. It nests in large colonies on clifftops in the Gulf of St Lawrence.

Previous page:
Quebec commands a magnificent position on the St Lawrence River. Founded in 1608 by Samuel de Champlain, Quebec is Canada's oldest city, and retains much of its traditional French charm.

Ontario

In the heat of a summer afternoon, half a dozen teenagers are leaning on an iron rail. Behind them stretches the endless expanse of Lake Ontario. Two of them are wearing yellow T-shirts emblazoned with a black fleur-de-lys and the name of Quebec.

The rail protects them from a 12-foot drop on to a grey, five-sided parade ground. They glance at one another and shrug their shoulders. Suddenly, a squad of young men in red jackets, black trousers and squat, peaked hats, each with a golden ball on top, march into view. They are carrying long slim rifles that Queen Victoria would have recognised. Like soldiers on parade everywhere, they move like machines and turn like robots. Eventually they form a square round two flags, the Union Jack and their company colours. With their cocked weapons jammed against their shoulders, they release a fusillade that echoes around the grey walls. Smoke drifts across the parade ground and the teenagers grin at one another. The show is over and they turn away.

Fort Henry, in Kingston, Ontario, was built in 1812 to protect the northern entrance to Lake Ontario from the marauding Americans. Now it is maintained as a tourist attraction for their richer, more benign descendants, and other visitors. It is part of a network of similar re-creations of historic settlements by which Canadians can profit from their past. The first National Historic Park, Fort Tom Howe in Saint John, New Brunswick, was designated in 1914 but the idea did not catch on. Only after the reconstruction of Williamsburg, south of the border in Virginia, began in the 1920s did attitudes become more sympathetic to conservation and then renewal. The Fortress of Louisbourg in Nova Scotia was first designated a national historic site in 1928 but it was little more than a half-buried ruin until 1960. After a royal commission pointed out that tourism could help revive the flagging economy of Nova Scotia, Ottawa authorised 25 million dollars to reconstruct the site.

Canoeing expeditions are very popular amongst modern Canadians. To lighten their loads when carrying their craft around rapids and other obstacles, some canoeists have returned to the Indian construction techniques which used thin strips of wood wrapped around a framework.

The pot that did not melt

Canada is a young nation in an old land. Some of its rocks are 2000 million years old while many of its families have lived in the country for just a generation or two. European settlers arrived in New France in 1608, but it was the end of the 19th century before the country took the trail that led to its present economic success.

Ontario lies at the heart of Canada, stretching from Hudson Bay in the north to the border with the United States in the south. Its industrial power and financial muscle are combined with natural resources that include vast forests, minerals of all kinds, including enormous deposits of uranium, copper, nickel and gold, and over half of Canada's best agricultural land. All this wealth has attracted people and Ontario's population has grown faster than that of the rest of Canada. By the late 1980s the province was easily the most populous in the country, with 36 per cent of the nation living within its boundaries.

The province's name comes from an Iroquois word meaning 'beautiful lake' or 'beautiful water', which is appropriate as fresh water covers over 68,000 square miles of Ontario, or about one-sixth of its total surface area. The name was first applied to the 7300 square miles of Lake Ontario in 1641 by European settlers. The lake receives most of its water from the other Great Lakes through the Niagara River in the south-west. The water flows out under the guns of Fort Henry into the St Lawrence River in the north-east. Almost a quarter of Canada's population lives close to its shores, while its western end is enclosed by the 'golden horseshoe', the manufacturing centre of Canada.

The first settlers to reach what is now Ontario in the 17th century were French explorers, fur traders, missionaries and soldiers who used the rivers in the south of the region as highways and built their cabins

In a vast country speckled with lakes, the floatplane is as useful as a taxi in a city. Whether carrying tourists or basic provisions for lumberjacks or isolated miners, the bush plane with landing floats is the cheapest, most effective way of travelling. After skimming the treetops for hundreds of miles, the pilots can land on even the smallest lake.

Tribes such as the Cree have learnt how to adapt their customary life-styles so that they are able to participate in the Canadian economy and welfare programmes without loosening their traditional social ties. These two Cree women are making bannocks, a kind of yeastless bread. The dough is rolled around green sticks and then baked over an open fire.

The moose is the most impressive of the deer family. The males can weigh over half a ton, while their branching antlers can extend to 6 feet across. The heavy and ponderous appearance of the moose is misleading, for this enormous animal has a turn of speed to match a horse. Found in wooded valleys, they feed on grass and young shoots when they are available, but will resort to mosses and tree bark in less fertile areas.

Canadians recreate their past by reconstructing early settlements such as Fort William. Skilled craftsmen repair or reproduce the weapons, tools and utensils that were once in everyday use. In this way they honour the first settlers.

on the banks. The British arrived in the north when the Hudson's Bay Company became established in Rupert's Land, named after the company's founder Prince Rupert, in the summer of 1670. They adopted a different strategy to the French and built trading posts at the mouths of the rivers that ran into the Bay, allowing the Indians to do all the hunting. The exchange of the furs for tools and guns developed into an elaborate ritual with the Cree tribe acting as middlemen for the Indians who lived deeper in the interior of the country.

Both European groups developed slowly during the next 90 years, with the French reinforcing their routes through Ontario to their trading post in the American interior on the Mississippi. The peace was disrupted when the British made their first successful attacks on the French forts in 1758. However, it was 1763 before British troops finally gained control of the region, a situation that was ratified by the Treaty of Paris in which France relinquished its claims to Canada. Many British soldiers decided to remain in the new land, but it was between 1783 and 1790, after the American War of Independence, when settlers loyal to Britain left New York State and Pennsylvania and travelled north, that the colony's

population started to grow significantly. The increase and the need to control the French-speaking settlers, the francophones, provoked a change to the local administrative arrangements. In 1791 the Ontario region became Upper Canada, with what is now the province of Quebec renamed Lower Canada. By 1812, about 100,000 people had crossed the border into the region.

Land was given to the loyalists and soldiers according to their rank and financial situation. Plenty of land was available for cultivation, but first it had to be cleared. Each colonist was issued with an axe, a hoe, a shovel and other necessary tools, as well as a gun for hunting.

In 1812, the border country of southern Ontario rang to the shots of the Anglo–American war that caused Fort Henry to be built. The Americans burned the provincial capital, York, later to be renamed Toronto; so the British put Washington to the torch. Armies marched, battles were fought and blood was spilled.

After the two sides called a truce in 1814, all the territory gained was handed back and the previous national boundary between Canada and the United States was reinstated.

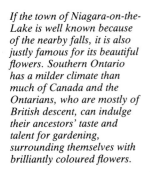

If the town of Niagara-on-the-Lake is well known because of the nearby falls, it is also justly famous for its beautiful flowers. Southern Ontario has a milder climate than much of Canada and the Ontarians, who are mostly of British descent, can indulge their ancestors' taste and talent for gardening, surrounding themselves with brilliantly coloured flowers.

Hard on the heels of the American Loyalists came the first major wave of immigrants from across the Atlantic, and by 1851 Canada's population was approaching a million. Most of Ontario's new settlers came from the British Isles and of these, 60 per cent were Irish. There were also many other Europeans. In Waterloo Region, about 60 miles west of Toronto, a large community of Mennonites – a Protestant sect that renounces violence and most modern inventions, and has links with many European countries – was established which has retained its identity to this day. German settlers were given land around Perth, close to the border with Quebec. Today, a dozen or so ethnic groups are represented and the whole province has become a cultural mosaic.

Unlike the United States, which has always been a vast melting-pot, Ontario – and the rest of Canada – has always encouraged ethnic groups to preserve their linguistic and cultural traditions. Of course, most Ontarians speak English, which is the working language, but many ethnic communities have retained their own churches or chapels, meeting-places and traditional festivals.

Every year since 1969, a week-long festival called the Metro International Caravan has been held in Toronto to celebrate the city's ethnic variety. Each community, Greek, Japanese, Irish, Italian, Hungarian, Ukrainian or whatever, sets up a pavilion named after the principal city of their homeland. These pavilions are scattered throughout the city and the organisers try to locate them near the homes of those who created them. Visitors buy 'passports' which give them admission to the pavilions and the entertainment and food that they provide. So it is possible to go from Budapest to Seville or Paris, all for the price of a bus fare. The International Caravan is becoming more and more popular because it provides pleasure for all the citizens while reassuring each community that it is not forgotten.

Toronto – the modern metropolis

Despite the vigorous expansion that has doubled the city's population in the last 30 years to make it Canada's largest city, Toronto respects its past. The suburbs have remained as small units, each with their own individual character, while the oldest streets have kept their beautiful red-brick, late-Victorian houses, usually two-storeyed and topped by gables. During the 1970s and 1980s, whole districts were restored to their former elegance. A passion for renovation swept the city and instead of everything being knocked down, the charming and slightly old-fashioned architecture was returned to its former glory. Once it was considered stylish to live in high-rise apartment blocks. Now the older districts are enjoying a second life, probably much grander than their first, for these houses, which were built for the respectable, are now occupied by the fashionable and the wealthy.

However, not all districts have moved up-market. Some with smaller houses have been taken over by the successive waves of Portuguese and Italian immigrants that started to reach the city in the 1950s and 1960s. These new Canadians, who are regarded as workaholics by more established residents, tackled the situation with such energy that their districts –

For a long time, Toronto was considered to be stuffy and unfriendly. Today it is one of the most dynamic and exciting cities of North America. The previously crumbling Victorian houses have taken on a new lease of life as cafés, boutiques or restaurants, reflecting the cosmopolitan origins of the citizens of the new Toronto.

This soldier's uniform is a vivid reminder of Canada's strong ties with Britain. Although a member of the Canadian army, he is in the service of the same sovereign as his fellow guardsmen in London. The regular parade of this élite unit outside the Parliament Buildings in Ottawa is very popular.

Like so many Canadian cities, Toronto is built close to water. But Lake Ontario covers an area about the same size as Wales and seems more like an inland sea. This allows its citizens to enjoy a range of water sports and to explore its extensive shoreline once the grip of winter has relaxed.

especially round the Kensington market area – have been completely revived.

Kensington market was originally purely Jewish but it is now very cosmopolitan, with small shops run by Portuguese, West Indian, Oriental or East European owners. It is full of bakeries, butcher's shops, cheese merchants, fishmongers and green-grocers and, with the addition of unique designer and second-hand clothing shops, it has become *the* place to be seen on Saturday mornings.

In the 1960s, Yorkville, another Toronto district, was the home of the city's bohemians, rather like Greenwich Village in New York or Chelsea in London in the 1920s and 1930s. But times have changed and Yorkville is now an elegant district with narrow streets, inside courtyards and charming cul-de-sacs, filled with boutiques, open-air restaurants and the other paraphernalia of affluence.

Of course, not all Ontario's weather is sunshine and flowers. The city takes on a different aspect during the winter months and when snow is on the ground the covered shopping centre, of which the Eaton Centre is a prime example, comes into its own. This huge, glass-roofed construction contains 300 shops on four levels and allows its visitors to shop in their shirt sleeves all year round.

Another modern building that has made a major impact on Toronto is the CN Tower. As the world's tallest free-standing structure at over 1800 feet high, its futuristic shape can be seen from all over the city. Built at a cost of 52 million dollars, it contains glassed-in lifts that whisk visitors 1120 feet to the skypod, which houses observation platforms and the world's highest revolving restaurant. The pod is surmounted by a 320-foot communications antenna that transmits television and microwave signals.

The building of Toronto's new City Hall in 1965 to a design by a Finnish architect marked a turning point in the modernisation of the Ontarian capital. The local architects were provoked into producing more imaginative designs and the city centre has become a model of its kind, filled with bronze or blue glass fronts reflecting the neighbourhood.

Farmers from another era

Toronto is not Ontario, just as New York is not the United States. Smaller communities dot the 412,000 square miles of the province, although most are situated in the southern quadrant sandwiched between the Great Lakes. About 60 miles from Toronto are the twin cities of Kitchener-Waterloo, which share two universities, several parks and a common past – the earliest German settlers and the Mennonite community, the first members of which arrived from the United States in 1786. This determined sect was founded in 1536 by Menno Simons and his strictest followers have kept its austere way of life, refusing to adopt any modern comforts – including electricity – and retaining a 19th-century style of dressing: long skirts, prefer-ably black, button boots and lace caps for women. On Sunday Mennonites take their families driving in horse-drawn carriages. Their farms are models of their kind.

Every year the twin cities host Oktoberfest, attract-ing 350,000 visitors. Many halls and tents are put up and all the participants dance in the best Bavarian tradition, downing outsized tankards of beer and stuffing themselves with sausages and sauerkraut.

In 1953 the small town of Stratford embarked on an ambitious project: a Shakespearean festival, which that year consisted of two plays starring Alec Guinness, performed in a specially constructed tent. The event was so successful that the tent was replaced by a series of buildings and the annual festival has become the most prestigious event of its type in Canada, running from June to October. A dozen plays are presented each season, with contributions from playwrights such as Chekov and Shaw as well as Shakespeare. The combination of an attractive set-ting, together with the outstanding quality of the productions, brings thousands of theatre-goers to Stratford every year to explore the local countryside and swell the town's grateful coffers.

Canada's capital, Ottawa, separated from the province of Quebec by the Ottawa River in the eastern corner of Ontario, has its own flavour that is different from the provincial townships and the metropolis of Toronto. Other Canadians used to think that its citizens were a little stuffy and intent on standing on their dignity. So when the capital became a centre of Canada's micro-electronics industry in the 1970s, their preconceptions received a jolt.

The capital also possesses some fine new amenities. Now the 800,000 people who live in or around Ottawa can enjoy the new Museum of Civilization and the National Gallery, two uncompromisingly modern buildings that stand on the banks of the Ottawa River and confront the more venerable Parliament Buildings nearby.

Ingenious artists have made use of any blank wall to decorate the older districts of Toronto with huge illusionistic paintings. This type of decoration was originally the work of a few artists who wanted to improve their immediate environment. But as it became fashionable, specialist firms have been established to do the work, turning some Toronto districts into stage sets.

Winter shoppers can stroll in their shirtsleeves in the Eaton Centre, which covers a large area in the centre of Toronto. Under an immense glass roof, a skein of geese seem to be flying through a summery atmosphere ideal for plants and flowers.

From Wabuk Point to Windsor

Ontario's landscape is very varied. Two-thirds of it is covered by the Canadian Shield, with rocks varying between 900 and 2000 million years in age. The soils that cover the rock are thin and low in fertility, particularly in the north near Hudson Bay, and are only capable of sustaining forests. Soils in the south, on the other hand, are very productive and the Niagara peninsula, wedged between Lakes Ontario and Erie, features orchards growing soft fruit, such as peaches, plums and cherries, as well as acres of apples.

Fruit-growing was established in southern Ontario by the Loyalist immigrants from the United States at the beginning of the 19th century. Then, in 1811, a Scottish immigrant, John McIntosh, found 20 wild apple trees on his farm in the east of the province. From them he developed the apple which bears his name and which today makes up more than half the total Canadian production.

The Niagara peninsula also produces grapes for the table and for pressing. Originally, Canadian wine-growers concentrated on the Labrusca grape which was suitable for making fortified wines such as sherry or port, but many changes have been made over the last few years and the old stock has been replaced with European *vinifera* stock, which makes better table wine. Every year at the end of September, the town of St Catharines near Niagara Falls holds the Niagara Grape and Wine Festival. This lasts for 10 days and is enlivened by concerts, sporting events and a huge parade with decorated cars and brass bands.

Southern Ontario also contains some of Canada's largest factories. Across the border from Detroit stands Windsor. Within a year of the opening of the Ford factory in Michigan, Canadians began to assemble Fords in Walkerville, a small town which has now been swallowed by Windsor. In 1876 the McLaughlin Company was established at Oshawa to build carriages and sleighs and in 1907 this company also began to assemble cars with imported Buick engines. Within 11 years, McLaughlin had been bought out by General Motors. Nowadays, car-making is still one of Canada's largest manufacturing industries, even if its business strategy is overseen from across the border in Detroit.

Keeping the arteries clean

Ice hockey is the national game of Canada, and although its popularity has taken it south of the border to the indoor arenas of the United States and across the world to eastern Europe and the Soviet Union, Canadians are still convinced it is their sport. Toronto has its own professional club, the Maple Leafs, which was started in 1927 and competes against the best of Montreal, Winnipeg and other major cities in the National Hockey League. As soon as they are old enough to put on skates, small boys dream of donning their club's colours. Few will be chosen to join the squad, but many manage to find places on one or another of the less-famous professional teams that are beginning to proliferate throughout North America.

Americans hate to admit it but their annual gladiatorial contest that culminates in the Superbowl started life in Canada. American football began when McGill University of Montreal challenged Harvard to a couple of football matches in the spring of 1874. The first was closer to soccer but the second

More than 40 houses, barns, workshops and churches were saved from submersion by the rising waters of the St Lawrence Seaway to create Upper Canada Village on a site near Morrisburg. It became a living museum of the colony in the 18th and 19th centuries, inhabited by guides in period costume.

Playing the part of a grocer's wife in the early 19th century, this Ontario lady carefully weighs out tea or flour, and counts sweets or plugs of chewing tobacco for the visitors.

*There is a certain irony in the visit of the blue- and black-clad Mennonites to Upper Canada Village to get a glimpse of the past.
They are the descendants of immigrants who came to Canada to live a life apart, renouncing all violence and much of the modern world.*

was played under rules that were nearer to the rugby then played in Montreal. The Harvard team were so taken by the game that they challenged Yale to a confrontation using the new regulations. The major American game has developed from the annual contest between these two universities. Interestingly, the Canadians have retained their own version of the game with a longer pitch, 12 men to a side rather than 11, and slightly different rules. Most of the big cities field a team that competes in the Canadian Football League.

That other stalwart of the North American sporting scene, baseball, has waxed and waned in popularity in Canada over the years. It attracted big crowds at the end of the 19th century, but later support tailed off. However, since the Toronto Blue Jays were founded in 1977, their entry into the American Baseball League has helped to revive interest in the game in Canada.

The Montreal Olympics in 1976 stimulated interest in a range of sporting activities that had previously lacked an attractive image for Canadians, and

Many different crops, from wheat to grapes plus a wide variety of vegetables, are grown on the highly mechanised farms of Ontario. Dairy and beef cattle are raised as well as poultry. The Niagara peninsula, in particular, is famous for the quality of its produce.

strenuous sports such as swimming, athletics, gymnastics and squash are becoming popular as more people realise the value of exercise. As in other Western countries, jogging attracts the health-conscious of all ages; and conditions are ideal for them in the beautifully kept parks which exist in nearly all the towns and cities of Ontario.

Education for all

Europeans tend to associate Indians with the West or the plains, but in Canada the greatest variety of native Indians are found in Ontario. Ironically the largest concentration, about 20,000 strong, live in Toronto. The remainder are more or less integrated into the white population, or in reserves administered by the Federal Government. They can be separated into two language groups. The smaller, the Iroquois-speakers, are concentrated in the south-west, near Kingston, while the Algonquin-speakers are scattered throughout Ontario. The largest tribe are the Cree, most of whom live in the north-west of the province.

Until the Second World War, the provincial government had difficulty providing schools for the Indian children who lived on reservations, which were situated in remote areas. The solution that was adopted involved placing the children in white settlements so that they could attend the local school. Because this meant that the children were separated from their parents, the effect on Indian families was very disruptive and the communities on the reservations began to disintegrate. However, after the Second World War the provincial government made a sustained effort to set up local schools on the reservations and this has helped to revive the Indian communities.

As for Ontario's other ethnic groups, the French-speaking Canadians – the francophones – only began to settle in the province at the end of the 19th century when, for various practical reasons, many Québecois emigrated to the neighbouring province. About 5 per cent of Ontario's students are francophones. Most of them are concentrated in the north, particularly in the mining towns of Sudbury and North Bay. In the past, the educational authorities provided French-language schools on a vague, pragmatic basis: 'when numbers warrant'. But in 1984 the Ontario Court of Appeal ruled that this was inadequate and that every student had the right to an education in his or her mother tongue. Minority communities are demanding with some success that the ruling be honoured.

Ontario's schools use a grade system similar to that in the United States. Primary schools take the children up to grade eight, from which most graduate at the age of 13. Secondary schools follow with grades nine to twelve, from which students graduate at 17 or 18. A thirteenth grade was necessary for university hopefuls but is now being phased out. After high school, 21 universities are open to students in Ontario, in addition to 29 colleges that largely offer vocational courses.

The real face of Ontario

Ontarians have a reputation among other Canadians of being rather conservative and a little arrogant, but that is perhaps a natural expression of resentment. Ontario is both the seat of national political power, with the Canada's parliament being located in Ottawa, and the centre of financial and industrial power through the importance of the Toronto Stock Exchange and the many businesses that are run from that city. This image is contradicted by the dynamism of the province's development in recent decades and the way in which it has enthusiastically accepted many new immigrant minorities. This appetite for change shows no signs of faltering and seems to indicate that Ontario will be a powerhouse in Canadian development for the foreseeable future.

Tobacco is among the most profitable crops grown in Ontario. For many years its annual harvest created a temporary flood of immigration at the end of August, as many students from Quebec crossed into the province to spend several weeks working hard, cutting and drying the plants.

Despite the prevalence of modern machinery on Ontario's farms, there is still a strong attachment to the working horses of yesteryear, which have their own competitions in horse shows.

Iqaluit, on Baffin Island in the Northwest Territories, used to bear the name of Martin Frobisher, the British sea captain who reached northern Canada in 1576. Apart from the Innuit (Eskimo) community which has always lived here, a few members of the Royal Canadian Mounted Police are stationed in the town, as well as meteorologists and aeronautical technicians, who work at the local airport.

Apart from the skill he must use to harpoon a fish, the Innuit fisherman needs patience. Motionless, his eyes fixed on the hole he has dug in the ice, he waits for a seal or an unwary fish to surface. Fishing and hunting remain the essential occupations of the original inhabitants of the freezing northern wastes.

The Canadian West

The story of the Canadian West is one of a transformation from isolation to integration. In 1871, when British Columbia was persuaded to join the Confederation of Canada, a journey from the new nation's capital, Ottawa, to Victoria, the capital of the new province, required considerable determination, stamina and time. On arrival, the traveller would have found a small town of about 8,000 inhabitants, with a few thousand more inland hunting for furs or prospecting for gold. Nowadays, a few hours in a jet will take that traveller's great-grandchild to a province of almost 3 million citizens with four universities and golf courses possessing velvety greens and manicured fairways. In 1871, the traveller had to use the American trans-continental railroad before transferring to a coaster to ship up from San Francisco. Nowadays, the direct flight passes over the vast Canadian wheatbowl and the oil derricks of Alberta before touching down at Vancouver.

Even today, the Canadian West is not over-populated. Only in the 1986 census did the number of citizens of the vast plains province of Saskatchewan finally pass the million mark. The same was true of Manitoba. Alberta has a population of about 2.3 million, many of whom were attracted by the oil boom of the late 1970s.

In all of these provinces, the people are clustered around the few cities. On the eastern edge of the plains, 60 per cent of Manitobans live around the provincial capital of Winnipeg. On the other side of the Rockies, the mellow climate of the south-western corner of British Columbia has attracted two-thirds of the province's population to the streets of Vancouver, Burnaby and Victoria.

Many of these city slickers are, in fact, only recent immigrants from the rural areas. The wheatlands have been turned into larger and larger farms as ever-increasing capital investment in new machinery has swallowed up the small producer in the quest for more effective use of the land, with no respect for tradition or sentiment. Even in the forests of British Columbia, efficiency is king. The power of the chain-saw and the hydraulics of the mobile crane have ousted the traditional sawyers.

One of the most exciting events of the famous Calgary Stampede is the chuck-waggon race, in which the contestants drive as skilfully as the first pioneers. They always seem to be heading for spectacular accidents but these seldom occur.

Canadians from all over the world

The ancestors of many Westerners did not come from either Britain or France, the traditional sources of Canadian immigrants. In the vast influx during the 20 years before the First World War, families from the Ukraine, Germany and even Iceland arrived in unprecedented numbers. In 1881, the area that was to become Saskatchewan held just 19,114 inhabitants. Thirty years later, the province had 492,432 citizens. The same pattern was true of Alberta, whose population grew from 73,022 in 1901 to 373,943 in just ten years. Manitoba has had similar growth.

Many of the communities that were established during this mass migration still live in the areas that they settled then. Thus, there is still an Icelandic community living on the south-western shores of Lake Winnipeg in Manitoba. However, these groups have not stagnated for they came to Canada to grow and prosper, which is just what their descendants have done. Nowadays, Canadians of British origin make up only about 40 per cent of the population of the plains provinces.

Every July, this transformation of the prairies is celebrated in Saskatoon, Saskatchewan's largest city. For seven days, what is claimed to be the biggest pioneer show in North America indulges in historic pageants, threshing competitions, vintage car displays, and livestock and agriculture exhibitions. However, as the original settlers of the area were enthusiastic Methodists, the reconstructed saloon at the centre of the festivities, which includes showgirls among its entertainments, sells soft drinks only.

Sailing and bicycling are the favourite occupations of the inhabitants of Vancouver. It rains a good deal during the winter, but there is never enough snow to interrupt the sporting activities. There are cycle paths everywhere to encourage young and old to enjoy the fresh air.

As soon as summer comes, tea parties are a daily event on the meticulously maintained lawns of Victoria, British Columbia. The population of the provincial capital is relatively elderly, for many Canadians retire there to enjoy the mild climate of Vancouver Island.

Away from the coast, the British Columbian climate is tougher and the winters colder. Even so, the weather is still milder than that of the prairies or the Maritimes.

The iron road

This invasion was only possible because the Canadian West had been penetrated by the railway. South of the border, railway mania had driven the lines as far as the American Mid-West as early as the 1850s, while the trans-continental link-up had been completed in 1869. This important connection was very much in the minds of the British Columbian negotiators when they were wooed by Ottawa, and they only agreed to join the Canadian Confederation in 1871 on condition that a trans-continental line was built north of the border within ten years.

It was one thing to agree to the condition, but another to make it happen. Funding such a project was an enormous problem for the Government because Canada did not have the financial resources available in the United States. Not only was the nation's 3.5 million population very small compared to the task in hand, but the track would have to stretch 1000 miles more than its American competitor, for, among other problems, the route needed to swing north to avoid the Great Lakes. Finally, in October 1880, the contract between the Canadian Pacific Railway and the Government was signed. The

last spike was driven into place in November 1885. The first train left Montreal for British Columbia the following June.

Although the Canadian Pacific was a private company, the project was completed only because the Government made a cash grant of 25 million dollars, land grants of 25 million acres, tax concessions and a 20-year ban on competition that might connect with the American system. At the time it must have seemed a formidable price to pay, but it clearly transformed the nation.

Nowadays the Canadian National Railway Company, like the American system, finds its passenger traffic an embarrassment. Over long distances, travelling by air is quicker and easier, while over short distances the car is more flexible. On the other hand, the railways cannot just abandon their obligations. The Americans have created a state-subsidised company, Amtrak, to run that side of the business. The Canadians have followed suit with Via Rail.

Freight, however, is a very different business. Not only have the goods carried by rail almost trebled in volume in the last 40 years, but new lines, sometimes over difficult terrain, have been laid to cope with the demand created by successful mineral exploration. The British Columbia Railway has reached the northern part of that province so that timber, as well as ore, can be shipped out. The Great Slave Lake Railway serves the same economic purpose in Alberta.

The Indians of the west coast of Canada are prolific artists. The bear, the eagle, the salmon and the beaver take on symbolic forms in their paintings and impressive totem poles. The Haida and Nootka call themselves 'the people of the cedar', from which the poles are made.

An Indian does not die; he goes on the 'long journey' to join the Spirits. In the past, bodies were laid out above ground in shelters, surrounded by their possessions. Nowadays, they are normally buried in cemeteries in which the graves are covered by possessions and protected by a shelter.

The most typical symbol of the west coast Indians is the totem pole, which skilled sculptors carve out of tree trunks that may be 60 feet high. They use red or yellow cedar which is easily worked and has the advantage of being extraordinarily resistent to rotting. This is why some totems set up 80 or 100 years ago are still standing, notably those on Queen Charlotte Island, off British Columbia.

The Indians show a respect and love for their old people and children, arising from their belief in traditional values and their confidence in the future of their race. In her little embroidered hammock, this baby girl has the place of honour in the family circle.

On Vancouver Island foresters still concentrate on cedars and Douglas firs, whose qualities make them ideal building material in a damp climate. It takes a chainsaw more than a yard long to cut down a tree this size, which will produce enough beams to make a medium-sized house.

Black gold and potash

Discoveries of previously unknown mineral wealth have changed the face of the Canadian West since the Second World War. The differences have been most obvious in Alberta since the Leduc oil field 'came in' during 1947. The wealth of the province increased dramatically in just ten years. The relative importance of Alberta's industries changed enormously as well. In 1947, agriculture was completely dominant. By 1956 the oil revenues were flowing in in unprecedented amounts, pumping vast sums into the construction business. Then, after the price of oil rocketed when the producer countries of OPEC took control of the petroleum market in the early 1970s, Alberta's economy was thrown into a frenetic caricature of itself as the boom soared to heights that were hitherto unknown.

It was not surprising that the recession in world markets, and the drop in the price of oil in particular, during 1982 and 1983 hit Alberta hard. Two Canadian banks folded. Matters were not helped when the price of wheat also took a nose dive. The land of the blue-eyed sheikhs had begun to look a little green around the gills. This dose of realism also helped to remind those in the business that the known reserves of Albertan oil, obtainable by conventional drilling, were such that there was only an estimated 12 years' supply left underground. Although the province has enormous reserves of oil-bearing tar sands, the cost of extraction and processing is so great that mining them is only worthwhile when the price of oil is high.

Cattle ranching still provides employment for many Albertans, producing exceptionally fine quality meat. The province includes many highly mechanised farming cooperatives, each as big as three English

Although they have a common border, British Columbia and Alberta are opposites in many ways. While Alberta has an income measured in thousands of millions of dollars from the sales of cereals and meat, it has been estimated that barely 3 per cent of British Columbia has soil suitable for agriculture. On the other hand, much Albertan timber is of such low quality that a forestry industry hardly exists. Across the Rockies, one of the world's great logging operations is so successful that their American rivals are asking Washington for protection.

British Columbia was originally called New Caledonia and the majority of the original European settlers did come from Scotland, though the province had been home for thousands of years to the Indian tribes encountered by Captain Cook when he made landfall there in 1793. When the province joined the Confederation in 1871, it is estimated that the Indian population numbered about 25,000. By 1986 there

While the smaller trees are still floated down the rivers, the larger logs of Douglas fir are delivered, these days, to the sawmills by huge articulated lorries which rush through the forests, driven by experts who handle them like sports cars.

counties put together, so it is not surprising that the Albertan rancher usually travels around in a truck, if not a private plane, rather than on horseback. But that does not prevent the West's traditional image from reasserting itself.

Every July, the cowboys of America gather for the Great Calgary Stampede, the prestigious rodeo that attracts competitors and spectators from all over the world. The events go on for a whole week, with competitors attempting to ride bucking broncos as well as bucking steers that are even wilder. They race 'chuck wagons' that are driven by yelling cowhands straight out of a Hollywood movie set. Cow-girls who have never seen the inside of a cowshed, except on television, are elected as beauty queens. Numberless country and western singers, as natural and wholesome as candy floss, settle on the city like a cloud of locusts.

Petroleum production in Alberta is developing in a new direction. Because easily accessible supplies of oil are shrinking, extraction from bituminous sand has started. To do this quickly and economically, enormous machines have to be built. Each cup on this huge wheel can scoop up two or three cubic yards.

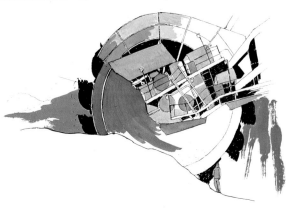

The annual Calgary Stampede, held during the second week in July, is the biggest rodeo in North America. Champions from all over the continent arrive for what is virtually a world championship. An enormous crowd gathers to watch the events, which all carry major prizes. Nobody goes around bareheaded – correct dress includes a stetson, preferably a white one.

The steer has only one object – to get rid of the rider, and the rider's aim is to stay on as long as possible. The time never adds up to more than a few seconds and the unseated cowboy must scramble to safety very quickly to escape the razor-sharp horns of the enraged animal. Most of the participants train for weeks before the start of the contest.

Logs and lumberjacks

Many of these new citizens work and run businesses in Vancouver and the surrounding urban areas. But British Columbia's most valuable industry is found far from the cities. Forestry dominates the province and has done for over 100 years. Logging began on Vancouver Island in the 1840s and, when the local towns began to grow, the industry expanded to supply building timber for them. The province also exported cut wood to the developing American cities farther down the coast. Once the railway was built, lumber was sent inland to help build the expanding prairie towns. Further expansion came with the opening of the Panama Canal, which opened the markets of Europe and the eastern American seaboard to them.

Success on this scale was possible because of the quality of the product. The coniferous trees of coastal British Columbia are the tallest, broadest trees in Canada. Douglas fir, the almost rot-proof western cedar, balsam fir, hemlock and sitka spruce grow very well in the mild, wet climate. During the winter, relatively warm air from the Pacific prevents the violent drop in temperature experienced in much of the rest of Canada. In the summer, the cold coastal waters moderate the heat.

The coastal water, much of which is protected from the force of the open Pacific by a string of islands, also offers an excellent, cheap transportation system for the logs. In calm waters, they are driven

were 66,500 registered Indians, but many more were integrated with the rest of the population. Those on reserves are mainly engaged in fishing, although during the last few years they have concentrated on reviving their traditional skills in carving, creating panels and totem poles from the omnipresent cedars, or building canoes and traditional houses.

The Indians are not the only minority to live on Canada's Pacific coastline. The first immigrants to arrive in any numbers after the British were the Chinese, who worked as miners in the middle of the 19th century. As the trans-continental railway approached completion, many more were brought from their homeland to work as labourers on the line's construction. They stayed on to create Canada's largest Chinatown in Vancouver.

The next to arrive were the Japanese, who settled in the south-west of the province as workers in the fishing industry. At one time many ex-servicemen and Indian civil servants retired to Victoria, attracted by the mild climate. In recent years another influx from Asia has taken place.

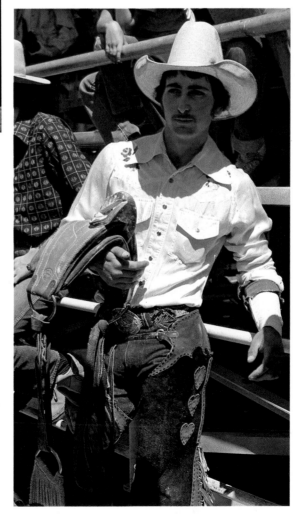

The competitors at small rodeos are cattlemen whose daily job keeps them in training for the contest. But at Calgary and in various other major centres, the cowboys are professional rodeo riders who earn large sums of money by taking part in 30 or 40 events a year.

together into large rafts, while barges are used to carry timber from the rougher waters of the Queen Charlotte Islands and the western shores of Vancouver Island. At first this shoreline timber seemed inexhaustible, but by the 1930s the lumberjacks needed to move farther inland to harvest the trees.

To move the cut timber, known as cords, to the coast, logging railways were tried – but the high cost of maintenance and the inflexibility of the route created problems. On the other hand, roads are very expensive to build in the forests of British Columbia because they frequently have to be blasted through solid rock and very large trees often need to be completely removed. Because the ground is rarely dry or frozen for predictable periods, as in many of Canada's other forests, the roads have to be surfaced to prevent them breaking up under the pounding they receive from the large trailers used to carry the cords. Care also has to be taken over water drainage patterns on the very steep ground to prevent erosion. If the timber was not of such high quality and so valuable, all these difficulties would have brought the industry to a halt long ago.

British Columbia is also rich in minerals. Coal and copper account for about the half of the annual value removed from the earth every year, followed by natural gas, oil, zinc and gold. Periodically, a spectacular discovery of the yellow metal will revive memories of the gold-rush days in a province where many still dream of a new bonanza. Of course, there is less oil than in Alberta, where you expect to find it gushing out of a tap in the bathroom alongside the hot and cold water, but the coal has provoked considerable interest in Japan, where it is being sold through long-term contracts to power stations.

In the south-west of the province, where the climate is particularly mellow, the quality of the soil has led to the creation of a flourishing fruit-growing industry. It produces some of the best crops in Canada, ranging from apples to grapes, as well as frost-vulnerable produce such as cherries, peaches, nectarines and plums of all kinds. The vast quantities of grapes grown led to the creation of commercial

The salmon of British Columbia attract large numbers of fishermen. Some try to catch their quarry at sea by trailing their bait behind a boat; but the most respected method is fly-fishing for steelhead, the king of salmon. Hours can be spent fighting a determined 12-pounder, which can break the line in a final desperate effort to escape. But nothing tastes as good as the fresh fish you have caught yourself.

Lake Louise is fed by an overhanging glacier and is only one of many such lakes in the Banff National Park, which sits astride the border of Alberta and British Columbia. In summer the alpine flowers turn it into a plant lover's paradise, while the lake is ideal for canoeing.

vineyards, which experienced one or two teething problems. In their initial enthusiasm, the growers, who preferred quantity to quality, tried to make wine from the wrong kind of grapes, which lacked sufficient sugar to produce fermentation. However, they soon learned from their mistakes and imported stock from Europe or California. Now the vines produce wines, especially some whites, which compare favourably with their Rhineland rivals.

Another industry that is unique to British Columbia is Pacific salmon fishing. The young are hatched in the rivers, then migrate to the sea where they mature. The adult salmon return to their home waters after two to five years, only to spawn and die. But before they enter the rivers, they must negotiate the large, modern fleet that assembles to capitalise on this annual bonanza. The value of the catch is so great that hydro-electric schemes that would affect the spawning patterns of the salmon have been postponed indefinitely by the provincial government.

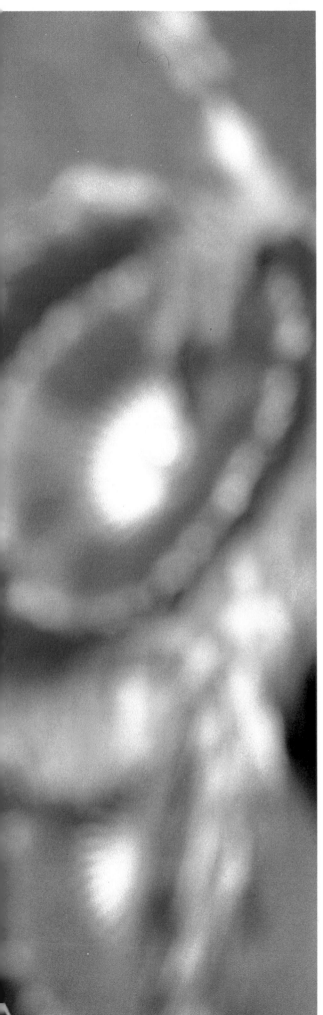

The scarlet force

In 1869, the British Government struck a deal with the Hudson's Bay Company. The Company gave up Rupert's Land in exchange for £300,000, 45,000 acres of land adjacent to its trading post and further unspecified land to be defined later. The directors were probably pleased because this sparsely settled territory had so far demonstrated its ability to sustain the fur trade and little else. Indeed, a report commissioned by the British Government in 1857 had thrown serious doubts on the possibility that a large section of the region would ever be anything more than desert. Nevertheless, the deal went ahead. Perhaps the British were influenced by the sale of Alaska to the United States by the Russians only two years before, and the possible threat to Canadian territorial integrity. Whatever the reason, there can be no doubt that British Canada came off best from the sale. What none of the parties could have known at the time was that a railway, a new variety of wheat and novel ways of cultivating dry land would transform what became known as the Northwest Territories into one of Britain's best buys.

In December 1869, the territory was placed in Ottawa's care. Canadian politicans soon passed the Manitoba Act, which sectioned off an area that is now only part of the modern province, next to the American border, centred on the tiny settlement that later became Winnipeg. Some time during the next few years, a variety of wheat known as Red Fife was sent to the area from the American Mid-West; it needed a shorter growing time than the types used previously. This was important, because the frost-free growing season on the prairies was relatively

The way of life of the Blackfoot Indians depended entirely on the bison before European immigrants arrived on the plains. They used its hide to make clothing and wigwams, or tepees. Nowadays the Indian reservations are used for ranching and farming.

The Blackfoot Nation is made up of three tribes that are spread among a number of reservations in Alberta and *across the border in Montana. They are the only group of Indians on the plains or hills which wears the huge* *plumed headdresses which people often wrongly assume are worn by every North American Indian.*

short. The first shipments of the new grain had to be despatched through the United States because the railway line from Montreal did not begin operating until 1886. But it was only a matter of time before the plains were settled and the people prospered.

One of the principal reasons why this settlement was so successful, so peaceful and so lacking in the dramas and blood-letting that characterised the same process in the United States can be summed up in one name: the Mounties. The North West Mounted Police came into existence in the summer of 1873 in an attempt to bring law and order to the newly acquired Northwest Territories. The first 150 recruits were sent to Fort Garry in Manitoba in August. Their first important action took place the next year after trouble between American whiskey traders and Canadian Indians in what is now southern Alberta. The arrest and conviction of the traders so impressed the Indians that their relationship with the Mounties never looked back.

During the next 15 years the Mounties did much long-term good in their work with the Indians, building up a climate of trust. In 1895 the police had the foresight to establish a small unit in the Yukon just before the Klondike gold-rush broke, ensuring that much of the disorder normally associated with such scrambles for wealth was avoided.

Over the years the Mounties changed their name and their function. In 1920 they became the Royal Canadian Mounted Police. But it was after the Second World War that their role shifted in a new direction as they became increasingly concerned with national security. They came to resemble more and more the American FBI. Not surprisingly, their involvement in such murky waters eventually tainted their reputation and, faced with the terrorism of the Quebécois separatists in 1970, they resorted to illegal methods that came to public notice.

Nevertheless, the force survives. Its present strength exceeds 20,000 and they police all of Canada except Ontario and Quebec. Their resources include eight crime detection laboratories, a fleet of patrol boats and an airborne section equipped with planes and helicopters. Their most important targets are organised crime, drug-dealing and large-scale fraud. However, it is their red coats, their horsemanship and their distinctive hats that are known all over the world.

The traditions of Europe and North America are intertwined in the outfit worn at the Calgary Stampede by this young woman from Alberta. Her dress stetson could only come from her ranching heritage, but her plaid waistcoat indicates that she is one of the genuine descendants of Scottish settlers who are entitled to wear the colours of their clan.

A little cabin in the hills

One of the big advantages of living in the West is the amount of space that is available for housing. Outside the centres of the larger towns, detached houses finished to the highest standards are the norm. Of these houses, 70 per cent have wooden frames, and standardised construction methods keep building costs to a minimum. The basis of the framework is a beam known as a 'two by four' from its cross-section in inches. These beams are set up in pairs about a foot or 15 inches apart so that, in the first stage of construction, the house looks like a cage. All the walls are hollow, making it easy to install electric cables or plumbing as well as insulation. The interior is finished with panels of plasterboard or plywood and the exterior with horizontal planks or decorative brickwork. The roofs are usually made of asphalt or rot-proof cedar shingles, which blend in with the wooded landscape.

The space created by the cement foundations is normally turned into a utility room. Originally it was merely a general store-room holding the boiler for the central heating, but once the house is finished the basement walls are papered, a few partitions installed and the living area is doubled. The basement frequently becomes the most popular spot in the house, with young people in particular. Here they can relax and put their feet up because, traditionally, the furniture is second-hand.

Log cabins are very popular with Westerners but they are usually only holiday homes in the mountains or on the shores of a lake. But even these rough, frontier dwellings have been taken in hand by the timber industry, and there are many firms in British Columbia that produce dove-tailed logs cut to exact measurements. All the new owner has to do is assemble his house like a set of Lego.

*During the 'Klondike Days',
the local people indulge in
typical American
entertainments: long parades
through the streets to
celebrate the past. ·Nowadays,
after the collapse in the price
of crude oil, the boom of the
1970s seems almost as remote
as the gold-rush and this
enormous 300-horsepower
car seems as quaint as any
19th-century costume.*

*The citizens of Edmonton,
capital of Alberta, enjoy
reliving the mad days of the
Klondike gold-rush in the
Yukon. Every year they
celebrate the anniversary of
this scramble for wealth by
organising a huge folk festival
which gives everyone a
chance to dress up in turn-of-
the-century gear and pretend
that they are setting out to
make their fortunes.*

Grain elevators mark out the line of the railroad in a country where the fields of wheat or barley seem to go on forever. Farming cooperatives unload their harvests into these towering storehouses before they are shipped in containers to less fortunate countries. A central office handles all the export contracts for the farmers.

The cultivation of fields of a size unimaginable in Europe has led to the creation of large and increasingly sophisticated equipment which is now exported around the world. The machines are normally owned by a cooperative or leased as it would be unrealistic for individual farmers to own a harvester which is only used for a few weeks each year.

for the tribe to which they belong. Altogether, they speak 50 different languages or dialects that can be organised into ten major linguistic groups. Living in the reserves brings certain inalienable rights, notably when it comes to hunting, fishing, taxes and education. These communities are increasingly asserting control of their own lives by creating self-governing bodies to run services previously managed by civil servants. This renewed confidence in their traditions and status has led to challenges to Ottawa that have taught the Canadian Government that it can no longer take Indian compliance for granted, particularly where their hunting grounds and reserves are concerned. No longer is it possible for pipelines and highways to be designed and built without taking Indian opinion into account.

Apart from the Indians and the Innuit, formerly called Eskimos, there is another group that has lived in Canada for hundreds of years and asserted its rights and traditions. These are the half-breeds, or *Métis*, who form a distinct group of 60,000 people in Canadian society. They owe their origins to the loneliness of the hunters and trappers of the 17th and 18th centuries, predominantly of French origin, who travelled the vast distances of the West for many years with only the native peoples for company. The children who grew up as a result of the liaisons between European men and Indian women developed strong traditions as a result of their isolation, which lasted into the late 19th century. And when they were finally confronted by the new Canadian nation, as its institutions spread across the prairies, they produced a leader who became one of the most charismatic figures of Canadian history: Louis Riel.

When the Northwest Territories came under Ottawa's control in December 1869, the only settlement of any size in these millions of acres was located near the American border in the Red River Valley. Centred on Fort Garry, the site of present-day Winnipeg, the settlers were predominantly *Métis* and their main lines of travel and communication were with St Paul farther down the Red River and across

The cooperative society which distributes the farming products also supplies fertilisers and machinery. As western Canadian farmers usually live considerable distances apart, a visit to the 'co-op' is an opportunity to meet and socialise. Everyone is willing to lend a hand in loading the 'pick-up', the small one-ton truck indispensable in rural areas. It is also an opportunity to exchange professional hints and local gossip.

The first Canadians

All of the West, whether it is now farmland, forest or someone's backyard, was once the preserve of a group of nations that we call by a single name. More than a million Canadians are descended from those first inhabitants: the Indians. Nowadays they can be found throughout the country, but they are most obvious in the west and north where many of them have kept their traditions and, in recent years, have taken much pride in asserting them.

In Canada, in order to be accorded Indian status and enjoy the rights that this brings, you have to be registered with the Government under the Indian Act. There are about 286,000 registered Indians, most of whom live in reserves that are kept exclusively

the border in Minnesota. So, when Ottawa sent its surveyors to plot the area without any previous consultation, the move provoked an insurrection. Riel, who had been brought up in the settlement but had gone to college in Montreal, soon emerged as its leader. When Ottawa despatched an aggressive expansionist to act as the settlement's governor, the *Métis* blocked his path. This led a group of Ontarians who had already settled in the area to challenge Riel. The *Métis* immediately denounced this as treason and one of the loyalists, Thomas Scott, was hanged.

Unfortunately, Scott was not only argumentative, but he was also a Protestant and an Orangeman from the Ontarian Irish community. Riel was a Catholic and a *Métis* who traced his paternal ancestors back to France. What had started as a local squabble now became Canada's first major political crisis, with Protestant Ontario baying for Riel's head while Catholic Quebec proclaimed him a hero of the people. It was in these circumstances that Canada's first Prime Minister, John Macdonald, performed a delicately executed balancing act.

A troop of British soldiers and Canadian militia were sent to assert Ottawa's authority. At the same time, a delegation from the Red River settlement was entertained in the capital while they conducted negotiations with the Government about the settlement's inclusion in the new Federation. As all the settlers' main demands were conceded and the Manitoba Act turned the region into a province, rather than the administrative territory originally envisaged, the Québecois saw the solution as a great victory for democracy, particularly as the Govern-

Before becoming the Royal Canadian Mounted Police the 'Mounties' were officially the North West Mounted Police, having been set up originally to maintain order in the far west. They are still very much in evidence there, where they patrol the highways as well as acting as local police. While performing those duties they do not wear the red tunics which are kept for parades.

In the western provinces like Saskatchewan, where homes are so far apart, socialising is a vital activity. Everyone gives parties but no host is expected to provide all the food. Instead, each guest contributes something.

Although picnics are family occasions, sexual segregation seems unavoidable. The picnic is frequently the only occasion on which informal groups can meet to discuss their common troubles, whether it is the government, commodity prices or the difficulties of shopping.

ment had agreed to recognise both French and English as official languages in the province and to establish French-speaking schools. Meanwhile, Riel had shown some discretion by slipping away across the border to establish himself in a new life as a schoolteacher in Montana, while Macdonald turned a politically expedient blind eye to the escape. However, that was not the end of the tale.

Fifteen years later, Ottawa's handling of the settlement of the West was causing considerable friction with those already in the territory. The announced tariffs of the soon-to-be-completed Canadian Pacific Railroad had caused an uproar. The Indians, who had been deprived of their right to hunt buffalo, were frequently close to starvation because of government penny-pinching and maladministration. The *Métis* in Saskatchewan had not received their promised land grants. To cap it all, the government surveyors had again antagonised the settlers by trying to draw neat lines across boundaries that had already been agreed

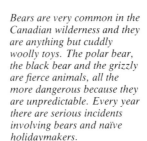

Bears are very common in the Canadian wilderness and they are anything but cuddly woolly toys. The polar bear, the black bear and the grizzly are fierce animals, all the more dangerous because they are unpredictable. Every year there are serious incidents involving bears and naïve holidaymakers.

locally. As a result, the West was close to revolt.

It was at this point that the *Métis* appealed to their hero to repeat his triumph. Unfortunately, the Riel of 1884 was not the man of 1869. Louis was convinced by what he believed to be a divine revelation that he was destined to found a new church in Saskatchewan when he returned in the spring of 1885. A provisional government was set up as soon as he arrived in the township of Batoche, but non-*Métis* support among the settlers soon melted away.

Back in Ottawa, Macdonald was still in office but he too had changed. Procrastination had replaced the decisive acts of 1869. But at the end of March a clash between the *Métis* and the Mounted Police, in which the settlers triumphed, alarmed the government and 7000 troops were despatched. Because they were able to use the newly laid lines of the Canadian Pacific to reach their destination rather than march there, the speed of the troops' arrival stunned the rebels. Soon they were defeated and Riel was in jail. Now the Protestants of Ontario resumed their cry for Riel's head, and this time Macdonald gave it to them. Riel was hanged on November 16, 1885.

In one man's lifetime, the isolated community of Riel's youth had become engulfed by the forces of integration. Those elements that helped to create the Canadian West – the railway, the immigrants, the Mounties and the faltering hand of Ottawa – also combined to end Louis Riel's life. But they did not stop his spirit. His fight for self-determination and minority rights survived him, and it too became part of the Canadian West.

Riding the white water in the rivers of Alberta and British Columbia in inflatable boats is both thrilling and increasingly popular. The vessels are virtually unsinkable. The oars are used only to guide the craft or possibly to slow it down, and there is also an outboard engine with reverse thrust as an additional brake.

The Far North

Above a line 60 degrees north of the equator lies Canadian territory in which a population similar in size to that of a provincial town rattles around in an area one and a half times the size of western Europe. The Northwest Territories and the Yukon Territory contribute 38 per cent of the Canadian landmass but only about 75,000 people, or 0.3 per cent of the country's population.

In popular imagination it is the frozen north, a barren, white wilderness, but the landscape and the weather are more complicated than that, and the wildlife is unexpectedly rich. Botanists have collected more than 800 different plants in the region; ornithologists have counted 75 species of birds; and the large animals include caribou, black bear, musk ox and whales.

The weather is most extreme in the Yukon because the province is sealed off from the moderating air currents of the Pacific by the Alaska Range, over the border in the United States, and by the lofty St Elias Mountains in the south-west corner of the territory. Back in 1947, a temperature of −63°C (−81°F) was recorded at Snag, a small township close to the Alaskan border. On the other hand, during a summer heatwave in Dawson, the old gold-mining capital on the Yukon River, the thermometer has reached a high of 35°C (95°F).

The Northwest Territories contain many enormous islands as well as innumerable smaller ones, and much of the land is relatively close to the various branches of the Arctic Ocean. This great thermal reservoir inhibits the wilder variations in temperature, which in a place like Baker Lake, just west of Hudson Bay, dips to −33°C (−27°F) in the winter and rises to 11°C (52°F) in the summer. However, in the more remote spots of the Mackenzie Valley, temperature variations can be just as grotesque as those in the Yukon.

The far north is divided into two large geographic regions: the taiga, a vast forest stretching into the arctic regions, and the rocky and wind-swept tundra,

where the intense cold limits the vegetation to a few stunted trees. At best, poor soil covers the underlying rock and only in a few select valleys can the roots of the vegetation extend into something more nourishing. This means that although 60 per cent of the Yukon is covered by forest, only 12 per cent of the trees are good enough to harvest. In the permafrost that covers the northern rim of the region, the soil is frozen permanently from 100 to 1000 feet in depth and only small plants such as lichen can grow and provide a source of food for the summer grazing animals.

During the short northern summer, this small Innuit girl can play with her puppy; but in a few months he will take his place in the sled team. In spite of the arrival of snowmobiles, some Innuit retain their dog teams.

The first settlers

This inhospitable land might have seen its first human inhabitants when Asian nomads crossed the Bering Strait about 25,000 to 30,000 years ago. However, it does seem more likely that they would have set off down the Pacific coastline rather than negotiate the mountainous terrain inland. In the generations that followed, their heirs spread through North America. A second Asian invasion seems to have taken place 10,000 to 14,000 years ago, towards the end of the last Ice Age. They also moved south to begin with – within 1000 years of their arrival on the continent they had penetrated as far as the southern parts of what is now Canada. But as the glaciers retreated and these ancestors of today's Indian nations increased in number, they followed the contracting icefields north. It was the vast herds of caribou that later drew them towards Hudson Bay and, finally, the Mackenzie Valley. The earliest-known traces of these people are to be found in the Bluefish Caves in the Yukon. Finally, in the last invasion across the Bering Strait 4000 years ago, the ancestors of the Innuit arrived, the people that are sometimes known in the West as Eskimos. With the land to the south already settled, they had little alternative but to travel east into the area now known as the Northwest Territories.

This pattern largely remains to this day. In 1987 the Yukon contained about 4700 Indians, roughly 25 per cent of the territory's population, and most lived alongside European Canadians in the towns and villages of the territory. The Innuit settled the mouth of the Mackenzie River, the Arctic islands and the

Baffin Island, three-quarters the size of France, is inhabited by a few thousand Innuit, concentrated in a few localities like Pangnirtung in the east. Their communities continue to thrive because they have incorporated such useful innovations as these small wooden houses into their traditional ways.

Bush planes are mounted on skis to enable them to reach isolated areas when the waters are frozen and the floatplanes cannot land. Thousands of these 'jeeps of the air' have been built. In the north they have saved many lives.

Innuit families are glad to get out into the open air and relax during the mild summer months. Because the sea-ice breaks up at this time of year, cargo ships can make their annual deliveries of non-perishable goods.

Arctic waters teem with a great variety of fish, including the famous Arctic char, a relative of the salmon. The Innuit usually catch it with a harpoon and then dry or smoke it so that it may be eaten during the difficult winter months.

If an oil heater now forms part of the traditional equipment of the inhabitants of the far north, the igloo still provides the ideal shelter when on hunting or fishing expeditions. In a few hours, one or two men can build this dome from blocks of hardened snow. The blocks are such efficient insulators that it is generally warmer in an igloo than in the wooden houses of the Innuit village.

north-eastern coastline as far south as Labrador. The 25,000 who remain here live in hamlets or villages and manage their own internal affairs through elected councils.

Although they live in wooden framed houses like the rest of the population, many Innuit still hunt for their living. Before the 19th century, the men had to find food or the family starved. After the whalers and trappers arrived, the Innuit turned increasingly to fur trading and used their income to buy food that was shipped in. The Second World War introduced extensive air travel to the north as defence, radio and meteorological stations had to

be serviced. Nowadays, the Innuit even have radio and television programmes in their own language, Inuktitut, beamed down by satellite, while few communities are without their own airstrip. The once essential kayaks and dog sleds have been replaced by motorboats and snowmobiles. Rather than undermine Innuit morale, these changes seem to have benefited the communities, if their health is any indication, and the people have an enormously increased life expectancy, even when compared to that of the 1960s. They have formed cooperatives to market their arts and crafts, which are now in demand among collectors in the West.

The Northwest Passage

The first immigrants to reach North America from the east were the Vikings around AD 1000, and recent archaeological excavations have begun to reveal how extensive their settlements and their travels were. The first recorded contact by Europeans with the people of the far north occurred in 1508 when a group led by Sebastian Cabot arrived in the course of their search for the route to Asia.

For 300 years, the quest for a northern route to the treasures of the East was a catalogue of frustration. After Frobisher, in 1576, and Davis, in 1585, got as far as Baffin Island, further serious attempts at navigation were abandoned until the 19th century. Parry, in 1819, and Davis, in 1829, were able to travel a little further west than their predecessors but they were still frustrated. The disappearance of Sir John Franklin in the ice in 1845 provoked more expeditions, none of which found Franklin's ship or the Northwest Passage. Only in 1906 did the great Norwegian explorer Roald Amundsen, who went on to beat Scott to the South Pole, accidentally find his way through. His journey took three years and it was 1944 before another ship, the *St Roch*, found enough open water to get from east to west in one season. The use of icebreakers helped to overcome this barrier, only to provoke another one: sovereignty. It was 1988 before Canada and the USA reached an agreement to allow US icebreakers access to Arctic waters on a case-by-case basis, and the question of sovereignty over the ocean is still unresolved.

Like their parents, Innuit children who have been barely weaned will eat raw fish and meat. Their diet is rich in proteins and fats to combat the cold, but it lacks vegetables and fruit, which are rarely available.
The administration of the Northwest Territories has set up a chain of schools for the Innuit children in which lessons are given in their language – Inuktitut.

The big strike

Detailed maps of the Canadian shoreline were one consequence of so many maritime adventurers sailing the Arctic waters. Exploration inland was concerned less with cartography and more with commerce. During the middle of the 19th century, fur traders from the Hudson Bay Company began pushing into the unknown regions of what became the Yukon. Gold prospectors followed them, moving up through British Columbia and into the Yukon as the century drew to a close. After one or two strikes of temporary importance, George Carmack, Skookum Jim and Tagish Charlie struck it rich on August 17, 1896 in Rabbit Creek, a tributary of the Klondike River, and precipitated what was probably the greatest gold-rush in history.

The lust for instant riches drew men from all over the world, but the Yukon of 1896 was not the California of 1849 and thousands perished in the brutal winter weather before they even reached the goldfields. The prospectors tried a variety of routes: some used the Pacific port of Skagway and tried to walk over the Chilkoot Pass, the trail immortalised by Chaplin in his film *The Gold Rush*; others used the port of Valdez and tramped through Alaska; yet another group used an overland route from Edmonton in Alberta. The city of Dawson appeared almost literally overnight at the junction of the Yukon and Klondike Rivers to service the prospector's every need. By 1898, Dawson had become the largest city in Canada west of Winnipeg, with proper water supplies, sewerage, electricity and telephones. At its peak it boasted 40,000 citizens; 90 years later its citizens numbered just 896.

Part of the Klondike's attraction was the location of the gold – in the creek gravels. No one who reached the site needed to mine for their wealth. All they had to do was stand in a stream and 'pan' for gold in the classic image of the Hollywood Western that would be created in the century to come. Between 1897 and 1904, approximately 100 million dollars' worth of gold was recovered from the Klondike gravel in this way. But by 1906 accessible

The seal is an involuntary collaborator in the survival of the Innuit. Its flesh provides food, its fat produces oil for lamps and its skin is made into clothes and boots. This animal, so essential to their existence, is central to many of their legends and myths.

Traditional Innuit life in the far north has inspired Canadians from the south. The annual dog sled-racing championship held at Yellowknife attracts competitors from far and wide. These races now form part of Quebec's carnival.

The sport of sled-racing has become so popular that the drivers now use specially designed trucks to transport their dogs between events.

gravels were worked out and extraction entered a more industrial phase with large machines and substantial capital investment.

Later 'strikes', although frequently as lucrative, were concerned with less glamorous minerals – lead, zinc and copper, the real moneymakers after the Second World War. However, during the early 1980s the fall in world commodity prices caused most of the mines to close, if only temporarily; even the vast lead and zinc quarry at Faro had to shut. When prices recovered in 1986 these mines were reopened and have since hit new production records.

The opening up of the Northwest Territories has been a matter of transport, as in much of the rest of Canada. The early settlement of Quebec and Ontario was based on the use of the river system. The West needed the railways to promote its integration with the rest of the country. The Northwest needed the aeroplane. Nowadays there are over 180 airfields, of which 14 are operated as licensed airports. Planes are fitted with floats or skis, enabling them to land on frozen lakes or water. These sturdy 'bush planes' have been specially designed to cope with the local conditions and are usually named after the local animals – Beaver, Otter and Caribou. Among companies intent on exploiting the mineral wealth of the territory, helicopters are increasingly being used to transport men and materials to distant locations.

The development of the region is very much a phenomenon of the last 40 years. In the early days it was merely a question of installing a few Mounties, setting up weather stations and medical posts, and establishing communications. Now the Canadians have established a new frontier, but its economic future is difficult to evaluate since so much remains to be done. Many research and development projects are being undertaken, several of them attracting international partners. By 1986 the value of the minerals exported from the territory was already over four times the worth of those minerals despatched by the Yukon.

However, the future of the whole of the Canadian North is subject to new forces as Ottawa transfers massive amounts of Crown land into the ownership of the native people and gives them over 1000 million dollars in compensation for the remaining territory for which they have now renounced claims. This land could prove very valuable in future as much mineral wealth is believed to lie beneath the surface.

In encouraging exploration and development, the territorial administration is treading a tightrope between economic growth and the ecological needs of the region. Despite the robust weather, the balance of nature is very fragile. The Innuit live in an intimate relationship with the environment, and pollution could upset a way of life that Ottawa has done much to encourage and sustain. Furthermore, the smallest upset in this region, which contains half the fresh water in Canada, could quickly assume the proportions of a national, if not an international, disaster. Extremely sophisticated techniques have to be used to monitor changes. Nowadays, an ancient life-style is protected by microchips and satellites.

In the far north the forests are thinner, the conifers shorter and deciduous trees rarer. In some regions, however, the soil does not freeze and the plants flourish in spite of the extremes of temperature between summer and winter, day and night. These forests are rich reserves of wildlife.

Quebec: New World, Old Charm

If you leave Quebec and drive north-east along the north shore of the St Lawrence, the opposite shore disappears and the river begins to look like the sea. Towns grow further and further apart – Malbaie, Baie-Saint-Paul. At Tadoussac you cross the mouth of the Saguenay, a wide river with towering cliffs. About 60 miles further on are two important shipping and industrial centres, Baie-Comeau and Sept-Iles: shabby towns that were disgorging iron ore yesterday but today are caught up in the worldwide steel crisis. In between there is no sign of life – no people, no houses. Beyond Sept-Iles, there is a road about 12 miles long that leads to an Indian village. After that, there is nothing.

You are entering the magic land of the north coast, the land of Gilles Vigneault, the Canadian *chansonnier* who sings so eloquently of its open space and the wide expanses of the sea. Only a few thousand people survive by hunting, fishing or seasonal jobs and government aid along the 370 miles of coast. They live in quiet, English-looking villages, with wooden railings and Presbyterian churches, Indian villages with French names like La Romane, or French-Canadian villages with Indian names, like Natashquan, Vigneault's birthplace. The families settled here 100 or 150 years ago and have not moved since. Sometimes two villages will be joined by a short road, but the big highway – always promised, often dreaded – that was supposed to link the hundreds of small rivers running into the Bay of St Lawrence, the route to Labrador and Blanc-Sablon, only exists in the Government's filing cabinets.

In modern Canada, a land of satellite dishes and giant hydro-electric schemes, the lower north shore is an anachronistic kingdom where the bulk of transport and household shopping is still carried by water: letters, cans of beer, videos and tinned fruit all arrive by boat. It is a land of imagination and a land of exaggeration, which can experience wild seas, or a snowstorm with visibility down to a few yards, or a sudden drop in temperature that refreezes the melting ice and traps a boat in a bay for 36 hours. Then the sun breaks through the clouds and suddenly the boat is moving between red rocks through incredibly clear green water.

Most of the province of Quebec is uninhabited. Above a line drawn about 300 miles north of Montreal there are no large towns – only northern settlements, like those of James Bay, and Innuit villages which resemble those of the far north. The climate is a big factor. In the mining area of Abitibi, the temperature averages about −16°C (−4°F) in January but can drop as low as −40 or −50°C (−40° or nearly −60°F). This creates a province split in two, in which the vast emptiness of the north is opposed to the urban concentration of the south, for the bulk of the population lives along the US border.

Yet by European standards a feeling of space remains, even in a metropolis like Montreal, where the most minor street is astonishingly wide. The smallest private house will have two or three storeys

The dramatic changes that have taken place in Canadian society during the last 30 years have made a profound difference to the lives of Canadian women. By the late 1980s they were taking over 55 per cent of all first degrees from Canadian universities.

and a lawn in front, together with a small back garden and a garage – neither of which is considered a luxury. All flats are spacious – only the district and the quality of the building will differ. There is even room in Montreal for cars. Most of the parking lots – including those in the centre – are open spaces, however, which does not improve the appearance of the city. In addition, under the energetic rule of Jean Drapeau, the mayor for over 20 years until the mid-1980s, Montreal acquired a motorway network which will have a dramatic effect on the city's appearance far into the future.

It is not only the province's roads that are built on the US model; the architecture too is very American, especially in Montreal. Only in Quebec City, founded in 1608 by Samuel de Champlain, have the old districts been preserved. Looking a little like Montmartre in Paris, it has long stairways running from the 'lower town' to the 'upper town' and, rare in America, several 17th- and 18th-century houses are still intact. Quebec City also has an atmosphere and a feeling of old France about it which makes it unique among the cities of the New World. This is in contrast with Montreal, where the old town, which was located close to the City Hall, has been reduced to a vestige of its former self. The residential quarters in the west of the city are more English in style and owned by well-to-do English-speaking families.

Montreal follows the classic American grid pattern of dozens of parallel streets. During the 1960s a complex of imposing skyscrapers was built in the Place Ville-Marie in the city centre. Nowadays, anyone arriving from the south and crossing the Jacques-Cartier Bridge into the city is immediately reminded of Manhattan. Demolition and reconstruction are a positive mania in Montreal. The area around McGill University and that at the foot of Mount Royal, which dominates the city, has been razed in the last few years, and while some of the replacements are attractive, others are less so. As a result, the three-storey houses with their exterior staircases and balconies on the eastern edge of the city centre, which are barely 50 years old, are beginning to look like period pieces.

Visitors to Montreal will be struck by its modernity rather than by its links with the past. Other than the skyscrapers, most noticeable among the innovations will be the way that the buildings of the city centre communicate directly with underground shops and entertainment, the vast subterranean galleries and

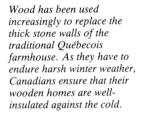

Wood has been used increasingly to replace the thick stone walls of the traditional Québecois farmhouse. As they have to endure harsh winter weather, Canadians ensure that their wooden homes are well-insulated against the cold.

the cleanliness – almost luxury – of the metro. If you do not have to work, you can spend all your time in Montreal without sticking your nose out of doors, which is an excellent arrangement in the winter months. On the American pattern, small shops have virtually disappeared in many districts. The local baker has given way to the big industrial producer, just as the open-air markets have disappeared under the advance of shopping centres.

When it comes to eating, the Québecois are ambivalent. They will readily make do with a club sandwich, fast food in a snack bar or a light meal at home. But at the same time, thanks to their French origins, the cities of the province have one of the biggest concentrations of good restaurants in North America. Only New York offers a more varied cuisine than Montreal, which has many French restaurants, several of excellent quality, as well as dozens of Italian, Greek, Chinese and Latin-American eating places. Such variety reflects the cosmopolitan population of the metropolis, which contains a series of substantial minorities. The Québecois is a great beer drinker, but he is also the biggest consumer of French table wine in North America. The French roots of the community are never far away, even if they are planted in American soil.

The Laurentians are among the oldest mountains in the world. Their proximity to Montreal has ensured that the wilderness has been tamed by the tourist industry and the region contains many fine hotels and restaurants. The attractive landscape is peppered with lakes that make excellent landing sites for the floatplanes that are necessary to reach the more remote areas.

In a country that contains over a quarter of all the fresh water on the planet, it is not surprising that fishing is such a popular hobby. This meal is being cooked on the Gaspé peninsula, a wide tongue of land sticking out into the Gulf of St Lawrence, which yields cod, herring, mackerel and Atlantic salmon. Spotted trout is caught inland.

The beaver, which is Canada's national animal, eats the bark of willow, ash and birch. Its lodges of logs and branches, cemented with clay are isolated in ponds created by the beaver, which dams streams.

Country and western – French style

In Montreal, then, the atmosphere is decidedly American. The night spots, whether for the young or the 'upwardly mobile', thrive on electric guitars, but there is also a 'Gasperien Casino' with a village band singing bawdy songs which reflect the traditions of the Gaspé peninsula on the Gulf of the St Lawrence. Outside Montreal and Quebec, bargain-price country and western records are sold by the thousands at rodeos and annual festivals.

Older traditions seem to have fared better in the small communities. Whether in a parish hall or the grill of the local hotel, the Saturday night hop has survived and modern music is giving way to square dances and jigs. Even if his instrument has been coupled up to an amplifier, the violinist will play the same rhythmic improvisations as in the past.

In the rural areas, traditions are still part of daily

life. Many Canadian stone houses have withstood the test of time. They are simple and sturdy rectangular homes with thick walls. The finest are probably in the richest farming areas in the east, the Richelieu Valley or La Beauce near Quebec. More modern houses are built of wood, with the traditional veranda running along two sides of the building where, in summer, comfortable rocking chairs can be set up. Nearer to the Gaspé peninsula, the architecture is more like that of New England.

Even more than the houses, the so-called Canadian furniture has survived to be treasured, although it only became fashionable about 20 years ago. The heavy country cupboards, kitchen tables big enough to seat ten-children families, and famous rocking chairs were piled up higgledy-piggledy in the farmhouses. Such furniture was either totally ignored, covered with successive layers of paint or relegated to the attic when everyone switched over to plastic laminates and chrome or 'Spanish-style' furniture. Over a period of years, experts and antique dealers made fortunes buying up households of furniture for a song from the unsuspecting inhabitants. But those days are over and 'Canadian furniture' is now classified and priced like the rest of the antique trade, with its elaborate catalogues, specialists and historians. Curiously enough – or by a natural reflex – the fashion for old Canadian houses and furniture, a growing interest in the past and a return to basics, dates from the 1960s and coincided with the emergence of Quebec from the wraps of the past.

Although improved communications and transport have done much to alleviate the isolation of the trappers and hunters, their life can still be as tough as that endured by their ancestors. This hunter, trapper and taxidermist lives in Abitibi, one of the coldest spots.

Hunting in Quebec is now strictly regulated as many indigenous species were hunted almost to extinction. However, it is still possible to hunt a large variety of game such as wolf, roebuck, caribou, lynx, coyote, skunk and, in this case, fox.

Snowshoes are much used in forests. Consisting of a light frame with varying degrees of lacing and thongs for holding the shoe in place, they enable the wearer to travel great distances over the snow.

Despite the deep snow, Thetford Mines does not come to a halt in winter. Situated between the St Lawrence and the American border, the town is the major centre of asbestos production. Most of the ore comes from open-cast mining, but there are also some underground workings. The area is surrounded by enormous piles of waste from the excavations.

For ten days in February, Quebec is taken over by groups of merrymakers celebrating carnival in a snow-bound version of the New Orleans Mardi Gras. The climax comes with canoe races across the ice floes of the St Lawrence.

1960: the rebirth

The Quebec of today is a very recent creation. Before 1960 – and the image is still very strong in many minds – Quebec was governed by an all-powerful Conservative Party, so traditional as to be almost immovable, and by the overwhelming presence of the Church. For all French-speaking Catholics, religious observance and Sunday attendance at mass were obligatory. The colleges preparing candidates for university were all directed by religious communities, and the principals of the Universities of Laval in Quebec and McGill in Montreal were both bishops. These two institutions specialised in producing lawyers and doctors, while the business world had been abandoned to the anglophones – those who spoke English. The Desjardins Cooperative movement and the two francophone banks were notable only for the modesty of their ambitions. The dynamic sectors of society and the economy were almost completely dominated by the anglophone minority – or assimilated into it – although it only represented about 20 per cent of Québecois

The snowmobile was the invention of D J Bombardier from Valcourt, Quebec whose company has now become one of Canada's largest engineering businesses. Mounted on skis with a caterpillar track to propel it, the vehicle glides swiftly over the snow.
Not only is the snowmobile replacing the dog sled in the north, it is becoming popular with sportsmen and has its own racetracks, ski-jumps and motordromes.

Artists from far and wide come to take part in the international snow sculpture competition that is held in the Place du Palais during Quebec's carnival. During the ten days of celebration a snowman, Le Bonhomme Carnaval, presides over the city as it enjoys popular concerts, ice hockey tournaments and banquets.

Ice hockey is the Canadian national sport. This violent game is a contest between two six-man teams, wearing leg guards and helmets against falls and accidental blows from hockey sticks.

population. In Montreal, in the banks, big shops or restaurants of the centre, French was hardly heard and was very much the poor relation.

If anyone had left Quebec in 1959 and not returned until 1965 they would not have recognised the place: the province had been transformed. The Liberal Party took charge in 1960 and 'the quiet revolution' came to pass. Monseigneur Parent's Commission of Inquiry completely overhauled the education system by advising the transfer of control from the Church to

the provincial administration. Medical insurance was introduced, and the first steps taken to establish a system of social security on the European model. Electricity was taken over by a provincial body and unions were established in the public sector. When the Liberals, out of breath and exhausted, lost power in 1966, the face of Quebec had been changed forever and the power of the Church had evaporated.

Today the colleges have been put into the hands of lay administrators and are attracting five times as

many students as they did in the 1950s. The hospitals are run by laymen and a new Québecois culture is bursting out on all sides. Quebec has discovered that it can produce and sell records, print books and even make films which are highly successful at the box office. At the same time, a new economy is beginning to take shape.

Inexhaustible natural resources

Quebec has few farms and very little arable land – 26,000 square miles out of the 595,000 square miles of the province. This contrasts dramatically with its other natural resources. The province's timber reserves, of which only about a quarter are being worked at present, seem endless – forests cover some 400,000 square miles of Quebec. Every year, about two-thirds of the forest harvest is processed in Quebec's paper and pulp plants, and the province produces nearly half of Canada's total pulp and paper products. In addition, Quebec exports large quantities of paper pulp all over the world.

As for its mineral wealth, most of the region is still unsurveyed, but the present long list of known reserves is impressive enough: 40 per cent of the Canadian supplies of iron ore; 24 per cent of its gold; 63 per cent of its titanium; 80 per cent of its niobium; and 90 per cent of its lithium. Quebec also has a large stake in a less attractive mineral: 36 per cent of the world's reserves of asbestos which, in spite of its carcinogenic properties, is still in demand.

If these riches appear to be precious assets for the

The Mistassini reserve near Lake St Jean is the home of the Cree Indians, who live by hunting, fishing and various handicrafts in its 13,000 square miles. Since the late 1960s they have asserted their right to self-government.

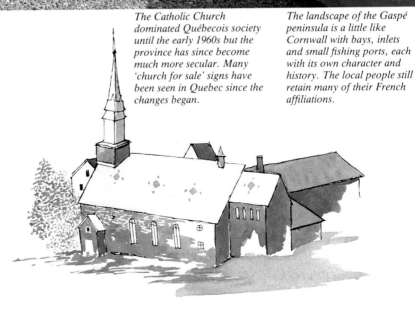

The Catholic Church dominated Québecois society until the early 1960s but the province has since become much more secular. Many 'church for sale' signs have been seen in Quebec since the changes began.

The landscape of the Gaspé peninsula is a little like Cornwall with bays, inlets and small fishing ports, each with its own character and history. The local people still retain many of their French affiliations.

future, they are also an indication of a problem that will have to be solved by the next generation. Quebec has to export its basic raw materials to the United States because it lacks the means to process them itself. To a certain degree this can be attributed to poor long-term planning at provincial level. Part of the problem is the lack of francophone managers in the extracting companies who could work with the local people; but the most serious difficulty is one of ownership and that is common to much of Canadian industry. Huge sections of the economy are in American hands. Not only is the automobile industry of Quebec owned by General Motors – most of its mining, chemical and electronic facilities are in the hands of multi-national companies. Even though the workers are well paid, the economy is lopsided and the province is forced to import manufactured goods from Ontario or the United States, although it is trying to rectify the situation.

Quebec's greatest asset is its abundant supply of power. Although there is no oil, there are unlimited supplies of electricity. The enormous hydro-electric project of James Bay on the La Grande River will have an output equivalent to 40 nuclear reactors when phase two is completed in 1990. Greeted with marked scepticism when it was originally proposed – before the cost of oil shot up – the huge project brought a storm of protests from ecologists and those

concerned with the fate of the Indians, because the barrages were going to flood huge hunting territories and create a lake the size of Wales, while the indemnities paid by the Federal Government by no means satisfied everyone. Compromises were worked out, however, and the Cree tribes in particular gained a new political maturity through the process of negotiation.

The project's momentum is now unstoppable. Quebec was already producing 40 per cent of Canadian electricity by 1986, and that was before most of the new turbines came on-stream. Electricity is already being exported to the United States and industries like aluminium, that need huge supplies of power, are becoming interested in locating future processing plants in the province.

At the time it was conceived the James Bay project was very ambitious, but it has caught the imagination of the world with roads cut through the wilderness, vast concrete constructions and northern encampments. It also has a symbolic value for the Québecois. For the first time on such a large scale, the province's resources have been harnessed and exploited by the Québecois themselves, through the state corporation of Hydro-Quebec.

The project certainly represents a spectacular success, but the horizons of local industry remain very limited. The case of Bombardier, the famous

The forests of Quebec cover an area twice the size of Great Britain, which explains the importance of timber to the economy. Forty-four million tons are cut every year, of which 75 per cent is turned into pulp and exported. The rest is sawn into planks or made into plywood.

inventor of the snowmobile, whose company is now an important constructor of large vehicles, is an exception to the rule. Québecois capitalism, whether public or private, is too frequently confined to industries that are contracting – like textiles or leather, for example. The development of growth sectors that could compete on the North American stage remain in the planning stage. In the meantime, Quebec's economy remains at the mercy of the American market.

Floating logs are a familiar sight on many Canadian rivers. A reliable and inexpensive means of transport, floating also helps to preserve the wood, since the prolonged immersion soaks out the sap and helps the seasoning process. Much of the wood is destined for the pulp mills, which are usually built at river mouths.

Until recently, the felling was done in winter by men who farmed in summer. Saws were used to cut down the trees, the branches were stripped and the logs rolled down the snowy slopes to the water. The arrival of the chainsaw and large tractors have made the process much easier.

My country is the winter

The standard of living in Quebec is slightly above the North American average. The province has about one car for every two inhabitants. Until recently, they were generally American models with a voracious appetite for petrol – for Quebec, like the rest of North America paid only a fraction of the price charged at the pumps in Europe. The Québecois are also the greatest telephone users in the world, holding the record for the average number of hours each of its citizens spends at the end of a line. They are also enthusiastic television watchers: there are two TV networks transmitting in English and two in French, one private and one public, two pay-as-you-view networks and one that concentrates on community programming, in addition to the many American stations that all Québecois cities can now receive by

cable. All this enthusiasm for indoor entertainment is encouraged by something the Québecois cannot change: the weather.

'My country isn't a country, it's the winter,' sings the *chansonnier* Gilles Vigneault, invoking one of the major forces governing life in Quebec. Even in Montreal, in the southern and therefore warmer part of the province, winter brings major problems. In the middle of Sainte Catherine, the city's main shopping

thoroughfare, temperatures can drop to −30 or −35°C (−22° or −30°F). And if the wind gets up, nobody can stay outside for more than a few minutes. Further north, near Quebec City, it is even colder. So it is not surprising that dealing with the cold becomes a full-time occupation.

In mid-November everyone fixes double-glazing to their windows, while cars are fitted with snow tyres and their radiators filled with antifreeze that will be needed for the next six months. Fur boots and overshoes are brought out of cupboards and are not put away again until March. An entire industry is built round the winter. Restarting frozen motors or digging them out of the snow is a money-spinner for the service stations throughout the province for, in spite of every precaution including electric block heaters for car engines, a morning always comes when the car refuses to start.

In town and country, an armada of snow ploughs and lorries stands ready for the first snowfall, the 'big storm' or even the 'storm of the century', which seems to happen every winter. All are natural evils, but they can be foreseen and are, therefore, more or less avoidable, though frozen or asphyxiated drivers and their passengers are sometimes found in cars stuck by the roadside or abandoned in ditches. In the main, everyone knows the rules: be patient, wait for it to blow over and stay where you are, either in a small country hotel or nearby friendly house.

In a big city like Montreal these superstorms become a little unreal. With the fresh snow nearly 3 feet deep on the street but with some drifts as high as a house, all traffic comes to a standstill. At metro stations in the suburbs, resourceful youngsters appear

The horse-drawn carriages on the narrow, winding streets of old Quebec City are strictly for the tourists despite the antiquity of the area, which has 18th-century stone houses with wooden shutters, steep roofs and many skylights.

The sight of these 20th-century gladiators on the streets of old Quebec is a typically Canadian surprise.

Many corners of Quebec retain the quiet charm of a French provincial town. This 17th-century house has been converted into a restaurant.

on their snowmobiles and offer to provide transport for desperate commuters. In the city centre, skiers glide along the roads and pavements and an unusual silence prevails. In this situation, it takes a week's thaw to get back to normal. Even without these extremes, snow is an ever-present hazard. The first usually falls in November, and it stays until the end of March under a slowly blackening crust that may not disappear completely until the beginning of May.

Although the Quebec winter can be a curse, it does not need to be a disaster. The town planners of Montreal have burrowed beneath the city's pavements to link the big shops, the stations and hotels, commercial centres and offices, providing miles of wide corridors, well away from the terrible cold. Quebec City is even more positive and holds a carnival in February.

Indeed, the whole province celebrates in a pre-Lenten binge and most towns of any size enjoy some form of carnival celebration. But it is in Quebec City that the fun has become a tourist attraction. Ice palaces are built and gigantic statues are carved out of the snow at the Place du Palais in a competition that attracts entrants from all over the world. A strictly local competition is held in the Lower Town. Parties of *traine-sauvage*, a type of crude bobsled,

torch-light processions or rides in horse-drawn sleighs are organised, as well as canoe races on the St Lawrence through the drifting ice. All of these activities are, of course, accompanied by strong drink, seen by many as the only way to fight the freezing cold. Some of the revellers certainly use it as an excuse to indulge in *grosgin* or *p'tit caribou*, a devastating mixture of sweetened red wine and pure alcohol.

Amid all this fun for the adults, the children are not forgotten. They have their own separate snow sculpture competition. They are also allowed their day at the Colisee de Quebec, the home of the Quebec Nordiques, the ice hockey team that represents the city in the National League. The youngsters take part in the annual International Pee-Wee Hockey Tournament.

Another favourite winter occupation is fishing on frozen lakes. A hole is made in the ice and a rough shelter put up as protection against the cold. Together with a few friends and a few bottles, you drop your line through the hole and the little fish cannot wait to take the bait on the dangling hooks.

Some streets in Montreal look as though they have been transplanted from Europe. The many skyscrapers of its commercial district, however, make it unquestionably North American. Built on an island 32 miles long in the St Lawrence River, it is crowned by the tree-covered Mount Royal, which is known locally as 'the mountain', even though it is only 770 feet.

Lakes by the thousand

Although the majority of the Québecois live in towns, nature always takes a part in their lives. Families of very modest means own or rent a country home, usually built of wood, near a lake in the heart of a forest. The lumberjack and the *draveur*, the raftsman who guided the floating logs down river, belong to the past, at least in their traditional forms. But the Québecois can revive these fading skills by joining a hunting or fishing party on a distant lake for several days, far from civilisation, on a men-only basis.

If the Québecois want sea and sand, they must cross the border to New England. There is plenty of fresh water in Quebec, 71,000 square miles in fact, but virtually no seaside resorts. Even if there were, the water temperature would repel any but those in rubber suits.

Much of this fresh water used to be in unsullied countryside. Even 20 years ago, simple villages still existed within 25 miles of the centre of Quebec. Today these regions have been sucked into the urban sprawl and the lakes, formed by the tributaries of the St Lawrence, are polluted. Holiday homes are now being built further north, at least 50 miles from the city, where unspoiled lakes, with only one or two houses on their shores, can still be found. Many of these lakes and rivers have been owned for generations by one or more families, or by fishing clubs. But the vast majority remain untouched and nobody squabbles over a stretch of beach or a patch of grass, or goes to war over a field.

Quebec's forests are still one of its most beautiful features, made up of conifers, birches and maples whose yellow and scarlet leaves turn the autumn to flaming glory in September. Furthermore, they are useful as well as a feast for the eye: they produce over 7 million tons of pulp a year for the paper industry. The picturesque *coureurs de bois*, the trappers, disappeared long ago, but the forests, which cover an area twice the size of the United Kingdom, do look exactly as you would expect. Nowadays, the remote glades still contain large herds of moose, as well as coyote, mink and wolves. Over 90 per cent of the forests are owned by the province, but they are exploited by private business groups who, as often as not, are American.

Many traditions are still alive in the rural areas. The end of summer corn-picking is one pretext for singing and dancing. Another big occasion occurs in

Shopping in Montreal also has a European flavour. As in the rest of Quebec, French is the dominant language but the city is very cosmopolitan with Jewish, Italian, Greek and Chinese districts.

Montreal is sometimes called the Paris of North America, but apart from the language it has little in common with the French capital. It is said that Montreal has more bars than most other cities on the continent and only New York has more restaurants.

the spring when everyone gathers at the 'sugar cabin' – a big shed, normally built of logs and located in the middle of a maple forest. This is where the sap is tapped and turned into syrup or sugar, providing another excuse for the city-dwellers to make an excursion into the country. Boiling hot syrup is poured on to fresh snow and eaten after being pulled into strands, well washed down with beer, all to the sound of a violin.

The sugar house is a good place to discover the rough entertainments of rural Québecois life, as well as its nourishing food, which often has a pork base that is meant to keep out the cold. Among the most popular dishes are pork and baked beans, pea soup and bread pudding. In winter, and particularly during the Christmas holidays, *tourtières*, round pies filled with minced meat and vegetables, rather like a Cornish pasty, are a popular choice.

When the maple sap rises in spring it is harvested to make syrup or sugar, providing an excellent excuse for a party. The sap is reduced by boiling and then poured on to snow piled on a table, where the party-goers tease it out, or 'pull' it with sticks.

The revenge of the francophone

The pleasure that the Québecois take in their traditions might well be seen as a search for reassurance at a time of radical changes in their society; for the fall from power of the Liberal Party in the provincial elections of 1966 did not signal an end to the drastic changes of the quiet revolution. It merely marked the end of the first phase in the total re-evaluation of the place of the francophones in Canadian society.

During the early 1960s an outbreak of Québecois nationalism had been bubbling up; for the first time, people talked of total political independence for the province. In 1963 the various groups formed their first important party, the Rassemblement pour l'Indépendance Nationale, the Party for National Independence. With the Liberals out of office, the leader of their progressive and nationalist wing, René Lévesque, took up the cause and proposed that the party adopt a more radical stand on Québecois sovereignty. When the Liberals rejected his ideas, Lévesque walked out and founded his own party. Within two years, this group had merged with others to form the Parti Québecois.

Meanwhile, Quebec society continued to modernise itself. The francophone majority began to penetrate the business world and struggled to establish its rights in Quebec itself. In 1967, General de Gaulle's famous cry, 'Vive le Québec libre!' had managed to embarrass everyone. But by October 1970 Québecois nationalism entered a more militant and dangerous phase when the Front de Libération du Québec, the FLQ, kidnapped Pierre Laporte, a minister in the provincial administration, after a series of terrorist bombings. The minister's murder by his abductors and the proclamation of the War Measures Act by the Federal Government in Ottawa, under which hundreds of Québecois were held for questioning, stirred the pot further. Yet, the Liberals, who had been returned to provincial power in 1970, were confirmed in office in the elections of 1973. It took the energy crisis provoked by the surge in the price of petrol, rampant inflation and a rise in unemployment to unseat them in the 1976 election.

Under Lévesque's leadership the Parti Québecois immediately carried out a series of radical changes to the provincial statutes of which Bill 101 was undoubtedly the most important for both Quebec and Canada. Montreal was, at that time, the largest city in Canada, with 60 per cent of Quebec's population. As time went by it was becoming progressively more anglicised: the local industry was financed by the English-speaking community and English was the language used at work, for publicity and all official pronouncements. As a consequence, nearly all new immigrants chose to learn English in the hope of getting on faster in their new country. The adoption of Bill 101 changed all that. French became the sole official language in the province of Quebec and all public announcements now had to be in French. Perhaps even more important, immigrants had to send their children to French-speaking schools. Finally, as far as immigration was concerned, Quebec was prepared to give preference to applicants from francophone or Latin countries.

Clearly, Bill 101 marks a turning point in the history of both the province and the nation. Despite

The sugar maple, whose leaf is the national emblem, turns to flaming colours in autumn. After a cold winter with heavy snowfalls, the tree is tapped to produce a fairly tasteless liquid in the early days of spring. It has to be boiled and reduced to make it crystallise into sugar.

Maple sugar and maple syrup are used for all kinds of dishes. Syrup is poured onto pancakes, tarts, fritters, scrambled eggs and even bacon, as well as a variety of cakes and sweets. Plessisville, about 50 miles west of Quebec, is the centre acéricole, *the headquarters of maple sugar and syrup production.*

its authoritarian nature, the Bill was probably the only way in which the haemorrhaging of francophone society in Canada could be stopped and the identity of 6 million Québecois in the middle of the sea of 300 million English-speaking inhabitants of North America be protected.

However, the short-term consequences were far from purely beneficial to the Québecois. By 1981, Toronto had succeeded Montreal as Canada's premier city and subsequent growth has only confirmed its pre-eminence. This has arisen because American executives chose to move their offices to Toronto rather than submit to the order that they must use French as the language of business. The consequent downturn in the local economy and the rise in unemployment probably made an important contribution to the Parti Québecois's fall from power in 1985.

Lévesque, meanwhile, had not rested on his laurels. On May 20, 1980 the voters of Quebec were asked to participate in a referendum in which it was proposed that the province assume greater responsibility for itself in economic and military matters. The idea was rejected by 60 per cent of the voters. Canada's Prime Minister, the charismatic Pierre Trudeau, himself a Québecois, then proposed a revision of the nation's constitution enabling them to determine their own political destiny and the return of the document from London to Ottawa. Despite opposition from conservative elements in the rest of

Canada, Trudeau forced the Bill through and the Queen travelled to Ottawa in 1982 to add the royal seal. But the Quebec Government under Lévesque refused to sign. Only after the Parti Québecois fell from office in 1985 and the Liberals gained control of the province were some of the matters resolved. In the Meech Lake Accord of 1987, Quebec took the first step in joining the new Canada.

The Accord emphasises the continuing importance of both the French and English lanuages to the Canadian people; the limits of federal spending power; an increased say in immigration policy by provincial administrations; changes in who appoints Supreme Court judges; and the rules governing constitutional amendments. As this will produce a major shift in the political balance of power between Ottawa and the provincial governments, some provinces are far from happy about the consequences.

The relationship between Quebec and the rest of Canada can still not be considered as finally settled. But the agreement between Robert Bourassa, Quebec's Liberal leader, and Brian Mulroney, the Canadian Prime Minister, over closer ties with the United States suggests a very different direction from that which the province has taken during the previous 25 years. Now that Quebec has something that the United States desperately wants – vast quantities of pollution-free, inexhaustible power – Quebec can assume its place in the sun.

This restaurant doorman in period costume symbolises the importance the Québecois give to a good meal in a pleasant setting, which is part of their French inheritance.

The Maritimes

The Maritimes are where the great Canadian forest sticks its finger in the eye of the Atlantic and reminds many Canadians of where their ancestors were born. It goes so far towards Europe that St John's, the capital of Newfoundland, is nearer to Ireland than to Winnipeg. But in a continent that is rolling over to face the Pacific Basin, such a geographical location can be a serious disadvantage.

Indeed, to many Canadians the Maritimes are the provinces that time passed by, an Atlantic backwater. Their highways and railways are roads to nowhere: an underpopulated region that has plenty of past but an uncertain future; a maritime sponge that sucks in federal dollars and manages to squeeze out plenty of excuses but few results.

However, the Maritimes did not always possess such a stunted and inaccurate image for, in the 19th century, they were a hive of activity that was much closer to the centre of Canadian life. In 1871, in the first census after confederation, the towns of Saint John in New Brunswick and Halifax in Nova Scotia each had more citizens than the millions of acres west of Ontario had settlers. Nowadays the position is reversed, and the population of British Columbia alone exceeds that of all four Maritime provinces added together.

Maybe Canadians find it easy to forget their Atlantic spur because so much of its business is internationally orientated and is despatched direct to its destination. Saint John is a major port and one of the few with access to the Atlantic that is ice-free all year long. It established itself in the 19th century when the New Brunswick timber industry developed as a result of preferential British tariffs and the extensive local river system, which made the transportation of the logs both easy and cheap. A shipbuilding industry, which used the wood, grew in tandem with forestry. This meant that 80 per cent of the province's economy was dependent on logging; as a result the economy began to sicken when three blows were struck at it: the demands for ship-building diminished with the advent of steel, the Americans erected a tariff barrier, and the West Indian economy – which had been a lucrative market – stagnated.

New Brunswick languished for decades until the province's wood pulp and paper mills had grown to the point where their substantial profits were filtering into the local economy. This boost to local business and the paper industry's need for more power encouraged further financial investment in hydroelectric plants.

Another change in business patterns came to Saint John's aid when many of the world's major shipping lines went over to containerisation in the 1950s and 1960s. This change speeded up the handling of cargoes and because the shipping companies had

The sea surrounding Newfoundland is one of the richest fishing grounds in the world. Such wealth has encouraged the French to hold on to the islands of St Pierre and Miquelon, seen here, as a base for their fishing industry despite an unresolved conflict with the Canadian government over their fishing rights.

invested substantial sums of money in their new ships, they looked to ports that could get their vessels back out to sea with the minimum of delay. This was to Saint John's advantage because, with the St Lawrence Seaway frozen in winter, it is one of Canada's few major ports with access to the Atlantic that is open all year. Nine lines use the container facilities to ship cargoes to over 100 countries.

Saint John is an attractive mixture of ancient and modern with a Martello Tower dating from the war with the United States of 1812 surveying the harbour from the west, and North America's first deep-water oil terminal, built in 1970, on the eastern shore. The centre of the town contains buildings from the 18th and 19th centuries that include the Old City Market, a covered arcade which was built in 1876, and Barbour's General Store which is decorated and organised in the style of the 19th century and includes a draughts board on which visitors can play the staff.

Being on the north side of the Bay of Fundy, which has very high tides, the harbour experiences a twice-daily surge which is funnelled up the Saint John River towards a deep, narrow gorge on the western edge of the town. Most of the time the river races over the rapids that fill the gorge and down towards the sea. However, when the surge arrives it rises above the level of the river at this point and flows back over the rapids, creating the impression that the river has reversed its direction.

New Brunswick is a small Canadian province but still covers an area equal to the Benelux countries. It is the most heavily wooded province with 88 per cent of its surface covered with trees and is surrounded by the sea on three sides. The early pioneers found the forests so dense that they had to explore the interior by water, which is why the valley of the Saint John River was first to be settled.

The silver harvest

The quality of the fishing around the Maritimes first drew Europeans to Canada in the 15th century. Nowadays, the industry contributes about 750 million dollars to the regional economy annually, or about 10 per cent of all productive industry. About 1000 communities along the Atlantic coast are largely or wholly dependent on the fisheries, with about half the fishermen being part-timers.

The offshore waters south-east of Nova Scotia and Newfoundland are one of the world's great fisheries.

The names of Marie-Eve *and* Isabelle *on these fishing boats in New Brunswick proclaim that the owners are French-Canadians. This is* Shippagan, *a busy, small Acadian port not far from Caraquet on New Brunswick's northern coast, an area famous for lobster.*

The different areas are known as banks and stretch from Georges Bank in the south, close to the American state of Maine, up to the Grand Banks of Newfoundland, immediately to the east of St John's. The fertility of these shallow seas is so great first because they are warmed by the Gulf Stream that flows up the Atlantic from the Caribbean, and secondly because, during the last Ice Age, the enormously thick glacial shield scraped off all the rich topsoil of Newfoundland as it gradually extended south and dumped it in the sea. This explains why the surface of this giant island is so barren.

The extraordinary productivity of these fisheries has been known for hundreds of years. Precisely when European fishermen first found them is shrouded in mystery, for those who discovered them were not inclined to share their potential wealth with their rivals. However, it should be noted that John Cabot, the Venetian navigator who landed on the 'new founde isle' in 1497 and claimed it for Henry VII, sailed from Bristol, and it was West Country fishermen who were among the first to acknowledge that they fished the banks.

As the next century opened, ships from England,

France, Spain, Portugal and Holland took advantage of this prodigious new source of food. There were two styles of fishing the banks. The English concentrated on working inshore from semi-permanent settlements in natural harbours on Newfoundland's south-east coast. Each spring, the captain of the first ship to arrive from England became the 'fishing admiral' and the source of all authority. The fish were caught close to the shore from small boats and unloaded onto the harbour wharf, where they were immediately cleaned, split and lightly salted. They were then laid out to dry on a 'flake', an open table that allowed maximum circulation of air. The cod processed in this way remained in good condition for months and were not taken back to Europe until the season ended in the autumn. They were known as the product of a 'dry fishery'.

The French preferred to work in a 'green fishery'. They had access to larger quantities of salt than their English competitors did, and they did not need to dry the cod to preserve it. This allowed them to process the fish at sea and return to port in France with the catch more than once a season. Some historians have suggested that these ocean passages by the English, French and Dutch fleets developed their seamanship to the point where they were able to navigate the world, and that the Newfoundland banks were the nurseries of empire. Nevertheless, despite these oceanic skills it was inevitable that the fleets would develop permanent onshore bases, which was what happened during the 17th century. The English and French settlements co-existed amicably enough, but during the first half of the 18th century the French lost almost all their territory in the region as a result of conflicts with England in Europe.

The only fragments that they still retain are the tiny barren islands of St Pierre and Miquelon, 50 miles south of Newfoundland. France is determined to hold on to these volcanic scraps because they serve as a base for the French fishing fleet, which catches about 20,000 tons of cod in the surrounding gulf every year. In 1977, Canada extended its territorial waters to 200 nautical miles, creating an exclusive fishing area that engulfed the French islands. This has created friction between the two countries that shows no signs of being resolved. To bolster its claim, France spends 25 million dollars on the islands annually, the highest per capita aid to any territory in the world.

The development of a new boat design in the 18th century, the schooner, changed the way that the banks were fished. These sleek sailing vessels carried dories, rowing boats with a high point at both ends that made them very buoyant. When the fishing grounds were reached, the dories were launched and used to catch the fish. This was achieved by the use of long lines with many hooks trailed in the water and baited with small fish or larger cod cut up into pieces. The catch was cleaned and salted on the schooner. These fast boats allowed the fleets to be based farther from the grounds than had previously been possible because they could cover the intervening distance quickly. Large fleets began to assemble, some of which were based in New England. This caused conflict with the British colonies after the Americans had won their independence.

The greatest of the schooners was the *Bluenose*, which was built in Lunenburg, Nova Scotia, in 1921. She was so fast that she won the International Fisherman's Trophy five times, only ever losing one race. By 1937, her fame was so great that she was honoured by the Canadian Government: her outline was reproduced on the reverse of the Canadian dime, a distinction she retains to this day. Unfortunately she was sold in 1942 and operated in the Caribbean,

Hockey generates such enthusiasm in Canada that children will play the game even when there is no ice, using a ball instead of a puck. As soon as the cold weather sets in any schoolyard or open space can be turned into an ice rink – all that is necessary is a hosepipe and a really frosty night.

Winters are tough on the Acadian coast and life tends to revolve around the warmth of the kitchen stove. This encourages the small gatherings of family and friends which have helped to sustain the traditions of the area in which folk singing is still very important.

In the Maritimes, patchwork is a traditional occupation which owes nothing to current fashion. When the first families arrived in North America, housewives had to practise the strictest economy. The smallest scrap of material was carefully hoarded and groups of women usually got together to create coverlets and cushions.

The blacksmith of Sherbrooke in Nova Scotia is practising the craft of one of his ancestors for the many Canadians who enjoy visiting their country's living museums. Sherbrooke is named after the English general who was the Governor of Nova Scotia in the early 19th century.

Part of the fortress of Louisbourg was rebuilt in the 1960s, using the original plans of what was once the capital of the French colony of Ile Royale, south-west of Cape Breton in Nova Scotia. Craftsmen came from France to help in the reconstruction and the site has become one of the most popular attractions in Canada.

where she was wrecked, off Haiti, in 1946. The Canadians so regretted the schooner's loss that in 1963 an exact replica was built in the original shipyard and named *Bluenose II*. Based in Halifax harbour, it is used as a tourist attraction.

The 19th century saw the banks fisheries at the peak of their power; but even at their height they were beginning to wither, smothered by their own complacency. Steel schooners began to replace the wooden vessels, which gave them greater strength and capacity. The Americans began running for home without salting their catch, developing a new market for fresh fish. The Great Lakes were also a developing source of fresh fish for the burgeoning market of Ontario. The Newfoundland fishermen responded by sticking their heads in the sand and keeping to the old ways. Yet, so confident of their situation were the 'Newfies' that, although they attended the Confederation talks, they chose to remain an independent colony and did not join the rest of Canada until 1949.

The conservatism of the fishermen living north of the border contrasted with the drive of their American rivals, and as decade followed decade their industry slid deeper and deeper into stagnation. Thus, when the new technology of fast-freezing appeared in the inter-war years, it was the Americans who took full advantage of it. Before long it had transformed fishing industries the world over.

Nowadays, 70–75 per cent of the Canadian catch is quick-chilled or frozen; 10–15 per cent is cured; and about 10 per cent is canned. Only the small proportion left is sold fresh. This processing more than doubles the value of the catch, a large proportion of which is sold on both sides of the Atlantic as convenience food.

By tradition, the profits are split after each voyage and distributed on the basis of shares. The formula for the share-out, known as the 'lay', tends to vary according to the size of the operation. On average in the Atlantic fisheries, the owner gets about 60 per cent and the the crew take the rest. However, the unions are very strong in the industry and the fine details are the subject of intense bargaining.

Before the Second World War the problem in the fisheries was under-investment and a lack of industrial capacity. But in 1947 the Canadian Government set up the Fisheries Prices Support Board and began pumping money into the industry. This programme helped the fishermen of Newfoundland once the colony became a province in 1949. The 1950s and the 1960s were the golden years.

However, even the rich banks began to flag under the intense assault on the fish stocks, and in 1974 the cracks began to show. The Government's response was a proclamation of the extension of Canadian territorial waters and the imposition of stock management programmes. Unfortunately, the large

More than 4000 inhabitants lived and worked in Louisbourg under the protection of a French garrison in the middle of the 18th century. In 1759 the fortress was destroyed by the British and the French community was dispersed.

fish-processing companies that had come to dominate the industry did not see the future in that light. They thought that the exclusion of the American fleets from home waters heralded a bonanza, and they invested so much money in the expansion of their facilities that the whole industry nearly collapsed under the debt. That meant that more federal intervention was necessary before the mess was unravelled. Fortunately, the shock has brought home the realisation that prudence and industry must go hand-in-hand with stock management, and today Canada is the greatest exporter of fish in the world.

The old painted wooden houses of the Maritime provinces always have a veranda on two or three sides where the local people enjoy their rocking chairs or two-seater swings from spring to autumn. In the winter it is a useful place to shake the snow off your boots under cover.

Cheticamp in Nova Scotia was established by 14 Acadian families at the end of the 18th century. It is now the home of a large French-Canadian community. .

The spruce of the eastern Canadian seaboard has always been popular with the paper industry because it grows so rapidly. This softwood predominates in the forests of New Brunswick.

Bracing breezes

Nowadays, the four Maritime provinces are no longer dependent on the fisheries and have diversified their economies, making a lot of money from tourists and from potatoes, minerals and timber pulp. By European standards they are far from small, but when compared to Canada's six other provinces, their scale is intimate. Indeed, in many ways they have more in common with American states such as Maine than with their fellow members of the Confederation.

Despite their proximity, there are plenty of distinctions between the four. The rich red soils of Prince Edward Island are a complete contrast to the meagre topsoils of Newfoundland and the New Brunswick uplands. The industrial vistas of Sydney, Nova Scotia, could not be more unlike the virgin forests of New Brunswick, which cover almost 90 per cent of the province. The rugged highlands of Labrador are quite different from the low, undulating coastline of Prince Edward Island.

'The shore road was woodsy and wild and lonesome. On the right hand, scrub firs, their spirits quite unbroken by long years of tussle with the gulf winds grew thickly. On the left were the steep red sandstone cliffs, so near the track in places that a mare of less steadiness than the sorrel might have tried the nerves of the people behind her. Down at the base of the cliffs were heaps of surf-worn rocks or little, sandy coves inlaid with pebbles as with ocean jewels; beyond lay the sea, shimmering and blue, and over it soared the gulls, their pinions flashing silver in the sunlight.'

This is how the most famous character in Canadian literature first sees the northern coast of Prince Edward Island. Anne of Green Gables was created by Lucy Montgomery who was born in 1874 and grew up in the area her character inhabits. Like Anne, she too lost her mother while still a baby and she was cared for by her grandparents because her father felt unable to cope with a small girl.

Growing up in the isolation of a farmhouse on the north coast, Lucy's dreams were her only playmates and once she was able to write, her desire to commit those dreams to paper soon followed. When she was 16 her father, who had moved to Prince Albert in Saskatchewan, married again and asked his daughter to join him and her stepmother. Lucy stayed for

almost a year but returned east because she was homesick. However, her experience was the stimulus for her first piece of writing to be published.

In the late 19th century there were not many career opportunities for respectable young women, so Lucy went to college and became a schoolteacher on Prince Edward Island. That did not stop her writing, however, and she learned to provide the stories and poems that the newspapers and magazines of the time wanted. In the autumn of 1901 she made a break and left the island for Halifax, Nova Scotia where she became a proof-reader and writer on the Halifax Daily Echo. From her letters it is clear that her new situation thrilled her but the need to care for her ageing grandparents drew her back to their farmhouse in Cavendish the following year.

The claustrophobic atmosphere of provincial life at the time became increasingly intolerable to Lucy and she satirised it gently in her most famous novel. She wrote about Anne in 1907 but the book was rejected by five publishers and she consigned it to a drawer for some months. Yet when it was finally published

The stunning colour of the maples of the valley of the Saint John River in New Brunswick announces when autumn has arrived.

Lobster fishing is popular all over the Maritime provinces, mostly as a private enterprise carried on by one or two fishermen from a small boat fitted with a winch which hauls in the heavy wooden pots. The lobster suppers of Prince Edward Island, many of them held in church halls, are a famous tourist attraction during the summer months.

In spite of much mechanisation, fishing remains a small local industry in Nova Scotia. The cod that makes up the bulk of the catch is usually frozen or eaten fresh – the old method of preserving the catch, salting, is becoming less and less popular.

the following summer, it went through six reprints in five months. Since that time it has sold almost a million copies in English and been translated into many languages. However, it was not until 1954, 12 years after Lucy died, that it was translated into Japanese. Since that time it has sold over 7 million copies in Japan and Japanese tourists make special pilgrimages to Green Gables, the old farmhouse she immortalised. It has now been turned into a museum and is surrounded by the Prince Edward Island National Park.

Halifax, the scene of some of Lucy Montgomery's youthful adventures, is very different from her birthplace. Facing on to the Atlantic, it is ice-free all year and a busy container port, like Saint John. However, it is also home to the Canadian Navy and its chief defence centre. The building of the naval dockyard was begun in 1759 by Captain James Cook, whose Pacific explorations are better remembered. He could see the strategic advantages of such a fine natural harbour, which is big enough and deep enough to accommodate the world's largest ships, in the North Atlantic.

Nowadays the city is a hive of activity with its own International Airport and a major freight terminal for the Canadian National Railway. It and its sister town Dartmouth, on the opposite side of the harbour, are the location of many branch offices of Canada's largest corporations. Together with the surrounding suburbs, they are the only urban centre in the Maritimes with a population of more than a quarter of a million.

Despite its current economic success, Halifax has conserved its past. It has taken care to retain and restore some attractive 19th-century warehouses which front on to cobbled streets near the harbour. The city still has two 18th-century churches and a number of military remains from the same period. However, when compared to St John's in Newfoundland, Halifax is very much the later arrival.

John Cabot was the harbour's first visitor when he anchored there in 1497. By 1583, when Sir Humphrey Gilbert arrived to declare that the island of Newfoundland was officially an English colony, the north side of the harbour already sported a small group of wooden houses. However, few early buildings survive because St John's was ravaged by five serious fires during the 19th century.

Much of St John's early history was wrapped up with the fishing industry but as the fishing vessels grew swifter and swifter and were able to travel farther afield, their home bases no longer had to be close to the banks. Small manufacturing industries became established in the city towards the end of the

Seal Cove on Grand Manan Island in New Brunswick is a typical village on the Bay of Fundy. Most of the men are either fishermen or lumberjacks, for the area is rich in timber. The buildings beside the water have been built on stilts because the tides can be high.

19th century and after Newfoundland became part of Canada in 1949, the provincial capital has become home to an increasing number of federal officials and their families.

Because the city is closer to Europe than any other part of North America, the Cabot Tower atop Signal Hill, just to the north of the harbour, was chosen by Marconi as the reception point for the first wireless signal transmitted across the Atlantic on December 12, 1901. For similar reasons a field behind the port was selected by Alcock and Brown as their take-off strip for the first non-stop flight across the Atlantic on June 14, 1919. Now the discovery of a major undersea oilfield on the Grand Banks suggests that this ancient settlement is set for a secure future.

The climate of the Maritimes is as mixed as the landscape. In Labrador, the weather is strongly influenced by the extremes of the Canadian mainland and the temperatures can vary as wildly as those in the Yukon. However, in the Northumberland Strait between Prince Edward Island and Nova Scotia, and in the Gulf of St Lawrence, the waters of the Gulf Stream have a moderating effect. In the summer, this mellow flow from the south meets the cold Labrador current and its icebergs. The result is summer fog, which drifts in from the sea to plague Newfoundland and Nova Scotia. The air currents are very disturbed where they meet, and in other seasons the area can be very windy. The worst-affected spot is undoubtedly the southern coast of Newfoundland and the mountains not far inland, where winds in excess of 100 mph are recorded relatively frequently.

None of these factors seems to inhibit the influx of tourists every year to the three more southerly provinces, with Nova Scotia alone receiving more than a million visitors every year. Clearly these holidaymakers would tend to be those of an active disposition, given the attractions that exist. Whether they wish to enjoy one of the many sports available – be it golf, fishing, sailing or even cycling – or to travel around learning about the area's past and taking pleasure in the natural environment, there are many alternatives available. Being one of the first areas of Canada to be settled, the Maritimes are strong on historical associations. One of the most interesting, particularly to French-Canadians, exists in Nova Scotia.

Dreams of Acadia

The first permanent European settlement in what has become Canada was made by the French when they established Port-Royal in 1605. The site, in the south-west of the province and now known as Annapolis Royal, is at the head of a well-protected basin off the Bay of Fundy. They called the region Acadia. Three times during the 17th century the English captured the Acadian settlements, but each time a treaty was signed by the Governments of the two countries back in Europe, and the territory was handed back. Only in 1713, by the Treaty of Utrecht, did France lose this base in the Maritimes to Britain.

Ironically, the Acadians thrived under their new masters; by 1750 the population had increased from 2000 to more than 12,000. In 1749 the British established a large settlement called Halifax on the Atlantic shore, for London was starting to flex its muscles as a prelude to an attempt to rid North America of the French forever. In 1755, while the two countries were officially at peace, the English made a number of attacks on the French forts that were strung out across the continent to protect the lines of communication between their trading posts which extended from the Maritimes, through the St Lawrence and on to the Mississippi. Only in Acadia were the English successful.

Prince Edward Island is known as the 'garden of the gulf'. Its family-sized farms produce enough cereal to feed the relatively small population, as well as fine broccoli, which is very popular in Canada. But the star crop is undoubtedly the potato, which is exported to the United States.

Then the local governor decided to use his own initiative. When the Acadians refused to sign an oath of allegiance, he took 6000 of them into custody and, without any authorisation from London, deported them to various French colonies and settlements in New England, the Carolinas and Virginia. In Louisiana they became the ancestors of the cajuns, an odd mispronunciation of the word Acadian.

After the end of the French and Indian War in 1763, 2000 Acadians managed to return to their land – only to find that, in the meantime, the English had encouraged immigration from New England and the Acadians had been dispossessed. Some were granted land on the far side of the Bay of Fundy in New Brunswick, while others took jobs in the fishing ports that lined the Gulf of St Lawrence. However, even at this point their tribulations were not ended, for when the American War of Independence was over, 14,000 Loyalists emigrated north to the area. As there were only 17,000 settlers in Nova Scotia at the time, the presence of the newcomers made a considerable difference, particularly since many of them had some capital. Their needs came before those of the Acadians, and again members of that community had to move on. Nowadays, only 3.5 per cent of Nova Scotians speak French as their mother tongue, but in New Brunswick the number is 32 per cent.

Of course, fishing and tourism are not the only important industries in the Maritimes. The success of mineral exploration in the rest of Canada since the Second World War has encouraged new surveys, frequently in very unlikely places. Thus, gold has been discovered in the holiday resort area of the Bay of Fundy.

Visitors to the Maritime provinces and particularly to New Brunswick are always amazed to find so many covered bridges on the highways. Sometimes 100 yards long, these wooden buildings are like a narrow barn that stretches from bank to bank. The shape creates a curious acoustic effect and children love singing inside them to hear the echo.

Charlottetown, capital of Prince Edward Island, is a busy place, mainly because of its position on the Northumberland Strait, from where vegetables – mainly potatoes – are exported. The citizens are employed in market gardening, tourism and a little light industry. The town, where the founders of the Canadian Confederation met, was first settled in 1720.

Traditionally, mining has been of scant importance in New Brunswick. Small-scale excavation of gypsum and granite took place in the 19th century and some coal was extracted. However, discoveries in the north-east of the province, in the Bathurst-Dalhousie area, completely changed the size of the operation. By 1986, 4000 men were employed in the mines which were producing 16 per cent of Canada's silver, 25 per cent of its lead, 9 per cent of its copper, 67 per cent of its bismuth and 85 per cent of its antimony. This development occurred in one of New Brunswick's poorest areas and has made a considerable difference to the local economy.

Nova Scotia has had a substantial mining industry for a much longer time than its neighbouring province, but it has largely been centred on one product – coal. This enterprise scored an early success when the type of ore excavated was found to be that needed by the developing steel industry. However, demand fell off after the First World War and was further depressed by the expansion of the oil and natural gas industries in the 1950s. That situation only changed after the revolution in oil prices in the 1970s. To contain the cost of energy production, the provincial Government began a vigorous programme of redevelopment in its generating plant. In 1978, 70 per cent of the province's energy came from oil; by 1986 it was down to 7.7 per cent, having been replaced by local coal.

Another novel development was the first tidal generating plant in North America, which was built on the Annapolis River. The tides on the surrounding Bay of Fundy are the highest in the world and create extraordinary effects. Some rivers at the top of the bay seem to flow backwards in the face of the twice-daily onslaught. If such power could be harnessed, the province's energy costs could be dramatically reduced.

The puffin is a familiar sight all along the Canadian coast, particularly in the east, where the colouring of its powerful beak during the breeding season makes it look like a bird from the tropical waters of the south. It is often found near colonies of gannets, looking like a philosopher in shirt-sleeves, watching their soaring flight in round-eyed astonishment.

Most Newfoundlanders are isolated from many of the opportunities that city-dwellers take for granted. This seclusion has preserved their life-style and a vocabulary that has strong links with the original settlers. The Dorset or Devonian dialect of 300 years ago, containing words long forgotten in England, can still be heard on the quays in the north of the island.

The only thing that the people of Prince Edward Island dig out of the ground is potatoes. The province has no minerals worth excavating on a commercial basis. However, the famous red soil is so fertile that potatoes can be harvested on an industrial scale and vast quantities are exported to the United States. Cereal farming is out of the question because the climate does not allow the islanders to compete with the wheatbowl of the prairies. One crop, however, does thrive in the cool, moist climate of the Maritimes: trees.

A paper revolution

Much of the prosperity of the region before confederation in 1867 was based on its forestry industry. The local boat-building industry used much of this timber and a considerable amount was exported. But as traditional markets languished and the better-quality timber of British Columbia was preferred by the building trade, the demand for local wood began to slide. Fortunately, technical developments in the United States and Europe were about to create

demand from a completely different quarter that would revive the industry in the 20th century.

Paper has always been made from cellulose fibres. Until the 19th century, the most convenient source of these fibres for the manufacturers was cotton rags. But, as the century wore on, demand for paper began to increase as a result of the growth of literacy and modern business practices. The development of paper-making machines in the 1820s had only made matters worse and pushed the price of rags even

Seen in the gentle morning sunlight, Port-aux-Basques seems to be the image of a peaceful small town. But when storms rage round this exposed ferry port in the south-west corner of Newfoundland, winds can reach 120 mph and trains have been blown off their tracks in the past.

The Bluenose *was the most famous Canadian fishing schooner and her profile is found on the Canadian dime. Built in 1921, she was the pride of the Nova Scotian fishermen and the fastest boat on the coast until 1936. But she was sold in 1942 and wrecked off Haiti four years later. In 1963 an exact replica was built in the original boatyard in Lunenburg.*

Although there are fewer shipwrights nowadays, wooden boats are still being built for the fishermen of Newfoundland. These boats are solid trawlers, able to stand up to Labrador storms and drifting ice.

Port-aux-Basques is a major port and fishing centre. The lobster-pots, carefully stacked on the quayside, are ready for the high season, between June and July, when the crustaceans are at their best. A good fisherman, alone or with an assistant, can easily bring in two or three dozen lobsters from each trip.

higher, for their supply was limited. The race was on to find a substitute.

Experiments with wood as a source of fibre for paper manufacture began in Germany in the 1840s, but another 20 years passed before the processes that had been developed could be scaled up to an industrial level. The cheapest way of obtaining the cellulose fibres from the wood was to grind up the logs. But the fibres produced in this way were too short to hold together effectively without the addition of other material, such as rags, to give the paper strength. The other problem was the product itself. No one could disguise the fact that paper produced from wood pulp looked cheap and nasty when compared to paper produced from rags, and its use met enormous resistance from publishers. Only in the 1870s, when the price of wood pulp began to tumble and the newspapers could no longer afford to stand aloof, did newsprint – as it came to be called – take over from rag papers for the world's daily press.

At first Canada was merely the source of wood for the paper mills of the north-eastern United States.

When this couple were born and raised, Newfoundland was not part of Canada. In the first referendum, held in 1948 to decide whether the citizens wished to become part of Canada, the Newfoundlanders said no. However, a plebiscite held the following year produced a small majority in favour.

But the early years of the 20th century saw two events change this state of affairs. First, the provincial Governments began to ban the export of pulpwood from Crown lands. Secondly, the American Government removed the tariff on newsprint in 1913. These two developments opened the way for the creation of a Canadian pulp and paper-making industry. Within ten years, Canada was the largest exporter of pulp and newsprint in the world, a position the country has retained to this day. Its largest market is the United States, which takes 52 per cent, while Western Europe takes about 12 per cent and Japan 5 per cent.

Travelling down the wind

The great forests of the Atlantic region, which still cover 77 per cent of Nova Scotia and almost 90 per cent of New Brunswick, are not merely a commercial resource for the paper-makers to harvest. They are also a haven for the extensive wildlife of the region.

Canada has become the biggest exporter of fish in the world in recent years. On the Atlantic coast the catches are mostly exported to Europe, although Japan is also becoming interested in the harvest of the Newfoundland Banks.

The Maritimes possess a wide range of habitats, many of them distant from human habitation and therefore safe from interference. This enables the caribou and the polar bear to maintain a foothold in Labrador. Other large animals include the moose, black bear, white-tailed deer and coyote.

One place where all the animals and plants should be safe is in the network of national parks. There are seven in the Atlantic region, varying from the wild cliffs of Terra Nova on Bonavista Bay on the east coast of Newfoundland to the red sandstone of Prince Edward Island, where just 7 square miles of marshes, ponds and sand dunes are protected. Even this small area is able to safeguard a nesting colony of great blue herons.

Without these animals, the seals, the caribou and the fish, man could never have survived in Labrador or Newfoundland, where Innuit settlements remain to this day. Without the cod of the banks and the pelts of the beaver, the silver fox and the mink of the mainland forest, the French and the English would never have endured the hardship and loneliness necessary to settle this vast and still half-empty land. Without the timber and the water power, the mineral resources, and the fertile soils of the prairies, who can say what kind of Canada would exist today? Its people have a lot to be grateful for and a lot to conserve.

Newfoundland is an island, but the province also includes a chunk of the mainland: Labrador. The shipping connection between the two has become increasingly important and the boats must be able to stand up to the savage winter weather. Until far into April, the waters of the Strait of Belle Isle and the 'front', as the east coast of Labrador is called, are strewn with dangerous ice-floes.

Gazetteer

United States of America

One of the visions that grips Americans is the sheer magnitude of their country, its great distances that impart a sense of freedom to take the breath away. For anyone who doubts it, there is Interstate 80, a double ribbon of highway that runs for nearly 4700 km (about 2900 miles) from New Jersey to San Francisco on the Pacific coast with never a traffic light on the way. Or the older US1 that stretches from the Canadian border to Florida; or the cornlands of the Mid-West like an inverted golden sky; or the huge sweep of the high western plains; or the mighty Mississippi river that drains half a continent on its 3779 km (2348 mile) journey from Minnesota to the Gulf of Mexico.

So vast a land is the United States that dawn comes eight hours later to its citizens who live on the westernmost islands of Alaska than to those in eastern Maine; even California is three hours behind the east coast. In the north there are Americans to whom the possibility of frostbite is an annual hazard, while in the south many of their fellow citizens grow palms and hedgerows of hibiscus.

In between these outriders stretches the great continent, embracing almost every kind of climate and terrain that the planet has to offer: polar tundra in northern Alaska and hot, sandy deserts in southern California. Oregon and Washington have vast coniferous forests, Florida has

mangrove swamps, and in the central and western states there are seemingly endless grasslands where the buffalo used to roam. There are ranges of snowcapped peaks such as the majestic Rocky Mountains and the Sierra Nevada.

The climate is as varied as the features and vegetation. Around the Gulf of Mexico it is humid and subtropical, while Arctic Alaska is intensely cold and arid. The western coast's rainfall decreases from north to south; much of it falls on the coastal ranges, resulting in deserts, such as the Mojave, farther inland. In direct contrast there is coastal California's Mediterranean climate, the cool, maritime region around New England and the continental extremes of climate of the central plains and western plateaus.

Despite its prodigious agricultural output, the USA is not primarily a farming nation. A century ago, about 15 per cent of the population worked on the land. Now no more than 1.5 per cent do so. The high yields produced by such a small work force are due to the 20th-century American genius for technology, which also turned most of the rest of the population into urban workers.

Always a trendsetter in industrial and sociological affairs, America seems to be heading for a 'post-industrial' future in which manufacture is based on automation and its people live in smaller, more widespread communities. Already, more than three-quarters of its work force are engaged in communications, the wholesale and retail trades, health care, banking and finance, government, catering, and in leisure and other services.

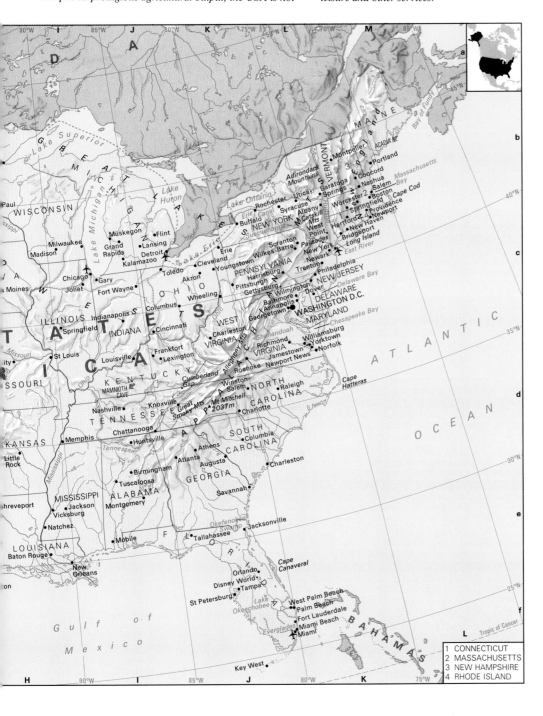

1	CONNECTICUT
2	MASSACHUSETTS
3	NEW HAMPSHIRE
4	RHODE ISLAND

USA AT A GLANCE

Area 3,618,772 square miles

Population 246,042,565

Capital Washington DC

Government Federal republic

Currency Dollar = 100 cents

Language English; many others spoken

Religions Christian (32% Protestant, 22% Roman Catholic, 2% Eastern Orthodox), Jewish (3%), Muslim (1%)

Climate Mainly temperate; variations include subtropical in the south, Mediterranean-type in southern California. Mainly hot summers, cold winters in north. Average temperature in Washington DC ranges from –3 to 6°C (27–43°F) in January to 20–31°C (68–88°F) in July

Main primary products Cereals, soya beans, cotton, tobacco, potatoes, citrus fruits, sugar cane, oilseeds, vegetables and soft fruits, timber, livestock, fish; coal, oil and natural gas, iron ore, copper, lead, zinc, gold, silver, molybdenum

Major industries Iron and steel, chemicals, motor vehicles, aircraft, telecommunications equipment, computers, electronics, textiles, forestry, paper and pulp, mining, fishing

Main exports Machinery, electrical and electronic goods, chemicals, cereals, motor vehicles, aircraft, soya beans, coal, instruments, petroleum products, small metal manufactures, textiles, tobacco, fruit and vegetables

Annual income per head (US$) 18,400

Population growth (per thou/ yr) 8.9

Life expectancy (yrs) Male 72 Female 79

Canada

A land of climatic and geographical extremes and a great diversity of peoples, Canada is the world's second-largest country after the USSR. The Trans-Canada Highway spans 8000 km (5000 miles) from Newfoundland to British Columbia, and it takes four days and five nights to cross the country by train.

Winter temperatures can dip to −62°C (−80°F) in the Arctic north, yet summer temperatures of 27°C (81°F) are commonplace in towns and cities to the south. In fact the southernmost part of Canada is at the same latitude as Rome and northern California. Most of the country's 25 million people live within a narrow strip along the American border. Almost two out of three live in Ontario or Quebec.

With nearly four-fifths of this enormous land uninhabited, nature lovers can readily explore vast stretches of unspoilt countryside or pitch camp where the only neighbours may be black or grizzly bears. Moose, caribou, elk and wolves also roam the wilderness, and the inland waters abound with salmon, trout, bass and pike. Canada has more lakes than any other country.

The huge network of rivers and lakes played an important role in opening up the country to the first explorers, trappers and fur traders. They were able, with only short hauls overland, to paddle their canoes from the St Lawrence river westward to central Alberta, north to the Mackenzie delta, and back again.

The first European settlers were the French. In 1605 they founded a community that is now Annapolis Royal on the coast of Nova Scotia, and in 1608 they sailed up the St Lawrence to the site that is now the city of Quebec. British settlement started two years later on Newfoundland. By the 1670s French explorers, missionaries, traders and trappers

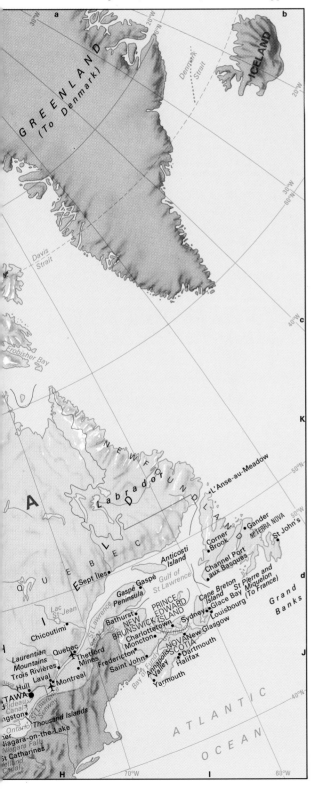

had penetrated west to the Mississippi headwaters and Manitoba. The British set up the Hudson's Bay Company to trade in pelts and furs, and the scene was set for rivalry between the two powers.

The French and British destroyed each other's settlements, each side recruiting Indian tribes as allies. The British navy raided French coastal forts, and French troops attacked British garrisons and trading posts. The issue was finally settled in the Seven Years' War of 1756–63. In 1759, a British army led by General James Wolfe routed the French in the Battle of the Plains of Abraham and took Quebec. The French surrendered Montreal in 1760, and the French colonies were ceded in 1763.

Despite Britain's military victory the country continued to support separate British and French cultures, languages and institutions. French settlers far outnumbered the British in Quebec and the surrounding area, so it was decided to recognise the Roman Catholic religion and retain French civil law and language (the Quebec Act, 1774). This separate system continues today.

After the American War of Independence (1775–81) more than 30,000 loyalist refugees moved north from the new republic to New Brunswick, Nova Scotia, Quebec and Ontario, increasing the population fourfold in many areas. From 1815 the British government encouraged settlers, and in the next 40 years more than a million immigrants landed in Halifax, Saint John and Quebec.

After the American Civil War (1861–5) there were fears that the strengthened United States might try to annex some Canadian territory. As a defence, the provinces of New Brunswick, Nova Scotia, Ontario and Quebec signed the British North America Act, creating the Dominion of Canada, in 1867. At the time, much of the west was in the hands of the Hudson's Bay Company, but in 1869 its territory was bought by the government, and overnight Canada tripled in size.

Two new provinces, Manitoba (1870) and British Columbia (1871), joined the expanding nation, the latter partly because it was promised a rail link to Ontario. The first line from the heartland to the Pacific (the Canadian Pacific Railway) was opened in 1885; the rail route eastwards from Montreal to Halifax had opened in 1876.

Prince Edward Island joined Canada in 1873, and Saskatchewan and Alberta in 1905. The development of railways and the purchase of the Hudson's Bay Company lands opened the Prairies to settlement and agriculture, and brought more European immigration.

The population doubled between 1900 and 1930. A lot of the newcomers came from central and southern Europe. Many of them stayed in the expanding cities and helped to give Canada its rich ethnic diversity.

In the First World War, Canada sent more than 600,000 men out of a total population of less than 8 million to fight in Europe. Canadians again hurried to the Allied side in September 1939. Canadians also fought in the Korean War and provided peace-keeping forces for Cyprus and Suez.

Many political institutions have British origins. Canda is a constitutional monarchy under Queen Elizabeth II. The Crown's powers are administered by a governor-general, now always a Canadian. There is a federal Parliament in Ottawa which has two houses. The House of Commons plays the dominant part. It has 282 members who are elected every five years. The upper house, the Senate, has 104 members who are appointed by the governor-general on the advice of the prime minister, and who serve until the age of 75. The two houses have similar powers, but all major legislation is introduced and first debated in the House of Commons. The Senate can veto legislation, but rarely does so.

CANADA AT A GLANCE

Area 3,851,793 square miles

Population 26,087,536

Capital Ottawa

Government Federal parliamentary monarchy

Currency Canadian dollar = 100 cents

Languages English, French

Religion Christian (47% Roman Catholic, 41% Protestant)

Climate Continental; arctic in north; maritime near coast (especially in British Columbia). Average temperature in Ottawa ranges from –15 to –6°C (5–21°F) in January to 15–26°C (59–79°F) in July

Main primary products Cereals, fruit and vegetables, livestock, rapeseed, tobacco, linseed, timber, fish; oil and natural gas, coal, copper, zinc, titanium, iron, lead, asbestos, nickel, salt, uranium, potash

Main industries Agriculture, forestry, paper and other timber products, food processing, iron and steel, engineering, mining, transport equipment, chemicals, fertilisers, oil and gas refining, cement

Main exports Motor vehicles, machinery, cereals and other foodstuffs, natural gas, chemicals, paper, crude oil and products, coal, metal ores, timber, wood pulp

Annual income per head (US$) 15,910

Population growth (per thou/yr) 8.5

Life expectancy (yrs) Male 72 Female 79

Picture credits

p.9 McHugh-Rapho; p.10 S. Held; p.11 left Vidal-Top; right Vidal-Top; p.12 Regent-A. Hutchison Lby; p.13 top A. Hutchison Lby; bottom Sioen-Cedri; p.14 Top; p.15 Sioen-Cedri; p.16 Sioen-Cedri; p.17 Rapho; p.18 top Sioen-Cedri; bottom Sioen-Cedri; p.19 right C. Zuccarelli; centre Sioen-Cedri; bottom Sioen-Cedri; p.20 S. Held; p.21 right Sioen-Cedri; bottom Sioen-Cedri; p.22 C. Lénars; p.23 McHugh-Rapho; p.24 left C. Lénars; right Sioen-Cedri; p.25 C. Lénars; p.26 C. Lénars; p.27 left C. Lénars; right C. Lénars; p.28 Haas-Magnum; p.29 Webb-Magnum; p.30 Spiegel-Rapho; p.31 top Yamashita-Top; bottom Sacks-Rapho; p.32 top Yamashita-Rapho; bottom Downman-A. Hutchison Lby; p.33 Webb-Magnum; p.34 Yamashita-Top; p.35 Yamashita-Rapho; p.36 Schofield-Liaison-Gamma; p.37 Schofield-Liaison-Gamma; p.38 Schofield-Liaison-Gamma; p.39 Schofield-Liaison-Gamma; p.40 Downman-A. Hutchison Lby; p.41 Spiegel-Rapho; p.42 De Roll-Top; p.42/3 top Yamashita-Top; bottom Sioen-Cedri; p.44 top J. Bottin; bottom J. Bottin; p.45 left C. Lénars; right Pasquier-Rapho; p.46 Pasquier-Rapho; p.47 top C. Lénars; bottom C. Lénars; p.48 Stock-Magnum; p.49 Buthaud-Cosmos; p.50 Vidal-Top; p.51 top Aurness-Cosmos; bottom Uzzle-Magnum; p.52 top Aurness-Cosmos; bottom Aurness-Cosmos; p.53 Aurness-Cosmos; p.54 top Aurness-Cosmos; bottom Burnett-Cosmos; p.55 top Burnett-Cosmos; bottom Harbutt-Cosmos; p.56 top Aurness-Cosmos; bottom Capa-Magnum; p.57 Godfrey-Magnum; p.58 P. Frilet; p.59 Aurness-Cosmos; p.60 C. Zuccarelli; p.61 top Rowan-Ana; bottom P. Frilet; p.62 C. Zuccarelli; p.63 Hartmann-Magnum; p.64 Champlong-Image Bank; p.65 Burri-Magnum; p.66 Vidal-Top; p.67 top P.G.H. Pix; bottom C. Zuccarelli; p.68 Hiser-Image Bank; p.69 Hinous-Top; p.70 Godfrey-Magnum; p.71 Jules-Ana; p.72 Morath-Magnum; p.73 Maple-Cosmos; p.74 Nahmias-Top; p.75 top Lowe-A. Hutchison Lby; bottom Downman-A. Hutchison Lby; p.76 top Lowe-A. Hutchison Lby; bottom Nowak-Top; p.77 A. Hutchison Lby; p.78 Gould-Scope; p.79 Godfrey-Cosmos; p.80 left A. Ernoult; right

Serraillier-Top; p.81 top Tiziou-Diaf; bottom A. Ernoult; p.82 Moisnard-Explorer; p.83 Marmaras-Cosmos; p.84 Perroton; p.85 top Belzeaux-Rapho; bottom S. Held; p.86 top Vidal-Top; bottom Fishman-Cosmos; p.87 S. Held; p.88 Perroton; p.89 Burri-Magnum; p.90 Moisnard-Explorer; p.91 top Ribieras-Explorer; bottom M. Breton; p.92 M. Breton; p.93 left Zuccarelli; right L. Girard; p.94 Gerster-Rapho; p.94/5 J. Bottin; p.95 Dunwell-Image Bank; p.96 Yamashita-Rapho; p.96/7 Kerdiles-Rapho; p.97 Manos-Magnum; p.98 Gamma; p.99 Burri-Magnum; p.100 Gamma; p.100/101 Gruyaert-Magnum; p.101 Hermann-Gamma; p.102 top Hermann-Gamma; bottom L. Girard; p.103 top C. Lénars; bottom Gamma; p.104 Gamma; p.105 top Michael Mirecki-Impact Photos; bottom Martel-Top; p.106 C. Lénars; p.107 Burri-Magnum; p.108 Hermann-Gamma; p.109 Gloaguen-Rapho; p.110 top Moisnard-Explorer; bottom G. Navarro; p.111 Remy; p.112 left Remy; right Varin-Visage-Jacana; p.113 top Government of Canada; bottom Government of Canada; p.114 Remy; p.115 left M. Bruggmann; right M. Bruggmann; p.116 Sharp-Image Bank; p.117 left Remy; right Remy; p.118 Koch-Rapho; p.119 top Maye-Atlas-Photo; bottom Cros-Explorer; p.120 M. Bruggmann; p.121 Government of Canada; p.122 top Zefa; bottom Zefa; p.123 Koch-Rapho; p.124 Taconis-Magnum; p.125 top M. Bruggmann; bottom M. Bruggmann; p.126 left Remy; right Bel-Pitch; p.127 C. Lénars; p.128 Vogel-Rapho; p.129 M. Bruggmann; p.130 top Molenaar-Image Bank; bottom C. Lénars; p.131 M. Bruggmann; p.132 Koch-Rapho; p.133 Valentin-Explorer; p.134 J-P. Martin; p.135 Koene-Explorer; p.136 left Remy; right M. Bruggmann; p.137 M. Bruggmann; p.138 top Aurness-Cosmos; bottom Aurness-Cosmos; p.139 Aurness-Cosmos; p.140 Aurness-Cosmos; p.141 top M. Bruggmann; bottom Aurness-Cosmos; p.142 Semeniuk-Rapho; p.143 Momatiuk-Eastcott-Cosmos; p.144 Remy; p.145 top Momatiuk-Eastcott-Cosmos; bottom Momatiuk-Eastcott-Cosmos;

p.146 Hiser-Image Bank; p.147 Momatiuk-Eastcott-Cosmos; p.148 top Vienne-Pitch; bottom M. Bruggmann; p.149 M. Bruggmann; p.150 Boizot-Explorer; p.151 Vogel-Rapho; p.152 Hussenot-Top; p.153 top S. Held; bottom Hussenot-Top; p.154 Martel-Top; p.155 top Martel-Rapho; bottom Martel-Top; p.156 top Deschamps-Diaf; bottom Pataut-Fotogram; p.158 Vogel-Rapho; p.159 Hussenot-Top; p.160 Maous-Gamma; p.161 top Giammetti-Gamma; bottom Thibaut-Explorer; p.162 Miller-Image Bank; p.163 left Duchêne-Diaf; right Peress-Magnum; p.164 Choisnet-Image Bank; p.165 top Burnett-Cosmos; bottom Schwart-Image Bank; p.166 Gloaguen-Rapho; p.167 Hussenot-Top; p.168 F. Kohler; p.169 Van der Hilst-Gamma; p.170 J. Guillard-Scope; p.171 J. Guillard-Scope; p.172 left J. Guillard-Scope; right J. Guillard-Scope; p.173 J. Guillard-Scope; p.174 M. Bruggmann; p.175 left M. Bruggmann; right M. Bruggmann; p.176 top Scotia-Image Bank; bottom J. Guillard-Scope; p.177 M. Bruggmann; p.178 Government of Canada; p.179 Zefa; p.180 Magruder-Image Bank; p.181 Remy; p.182 Cochrane-Rapho; p.183 M. Bruggmann; p.184 top Cochrane-Rapho; bottom Van der Hilst-Gamma; p.185 M. Bruggmann; p.186 Van der Hilst-Gamma; p.187 Gleizes-Explorer

Front cover
Top: Mike Andrews-Susan Grigg Agency; Bottom: E. Hummel-ZEFA

74-002-1